HE HAS MADE ME GLAD

Printed and bound in Great Britain by
CPI Antony Rowe, Chippenham and Eastbourne

Published by Crossbridge Books
Tree Shadow, Berrow Green
Martley, WR6 6PL
Tel: +44 (0)1886 821128   www.crossbridgebooks.com

First published 2009

ISBN 978-0-9561787-2-5

British Library Cataloguing in Publication Data.
A catalogue record for this book is available from
the British Library.

Also published by Crossbridge Books:

It's True! Trevor Dearing
Total Healing Trevor Dearing
The God of Miracles Trevor and Anne Dearing
Schizophrenia Defeated James Stacey
Mountains on the Moon Michael Arthern

BIBLICAL QUOTATIONS
Many are from the Authorised, or King James Version (KJV); some are
from the Revised Standard Version (RSV) and some from the
New International Version (NIV).

HE HAS MADE ME GLAD

GLAD ROSIE

CROSSBRIDGE BOOKS

Preface

On a number of occasions over the years I have been asked to share my testimony of my experience as a Christian. Frequently after I have shared what the Lord has done in and through me someone would come to me and say, "You ought to write a book." This has happened so often that I have wondered if the Lord was in such remarks or whether it was just something 'nice' that they wanted to say. There came a point when I prayed, "Lord, if You want me to write a book about my experience of You, lead someone to say so after the next time I share my testimony." Soon such a request came and I prayed, "Lord, if You want me to write this book then give me the sign." The meeting took place and the comment came, "You ought to write a book"!

When I retired from the full time ministry I decided to write my story. It is not my husband Bill's story though, inevitably, because our lives are so bound together, a lot of his story comes in. Neither is it our children's story though they, too, come into my story. I do not write for any financial gain as any income from the sale of this book will be given away. I write in simple obedience to my Lord. It is God's Story as revealed in my life and what I write is for His Glory. May it encourage you in your walk with the Lord.

Contents

"You have been saved for a purpose ..."

We were standing in the living room, my mother, my brother David (22 months my junior) baby Harry crawling on the floor and myself. The doctor, having been called out for one of the others, was about to leave.

"Is that the child who had meningitis?" he asked.

Mum replied, "Yes."

"How's she doing at school?"

I knew what lay behind his question. In those days there was no cure for meningitis. If one did survive, it left its mark somewhere – the eyes affected by blindness, ears became deaf, the brain retarded. The doctor could see I was all right physically but he wanted to know about my mental state. Although I had missed a lot of school through ill health my mother told him I was high up in my class.

"It's a miracle," he said, "a miracle!"

From early childhood my mother told me, "You have been saved for a purpose." I don't believe I'm any different from anyone else. We're all here for a purpose – but it is wonderful to be told so. I grew up wondering what that purpose was.

One day I was walking down the road and I thought of Jesus. "He is God's Son," I thought to myself. "Why didn't He have a daughter? Perhaps He has! Why shouldn't it be me?" It wasn't that I had an over-inflated ego, in fact I felt insignificant and shy, but I knew I was special to God. Why had He saved me from death, not once but several times? What was His purpose for me?

1

"Who do you think you are?"

The two strands that came together to make me could not have been more different. Dad was of a travelling Bohemian theatrical family and Mum from solid Midland Methodist background! To start three generations back, on my mother's side, great-grandfather Middleton was a carrier in the village of Abthorpe in Northants. A Methodist, he was almost Quaker-like in his insistence that only God was to be shown respect above others. It was the custom in the village that girls curtseyed to the vicar, but great-grandfather forbade his daughters to do so. "He's only a man. You are not to curtsey to him." He was an important man in the village, being a special link between the villagers and the outside world. He brought in letters and parcels and on Saturdays everyone was eager to see the titbits brought in for the weekend – maybe a piece of bacon for the Sunday table!

His son Harry, my grandfather, was a staunch Primitive Methodist, and faithfulness to God meant faithfulness to Primitive Methodism. In the 1920s moves were made to unite the Primitive and Wesleyan Methodists. Each member was asked to vote on whether they wanted to unite or remain separate. My mother was a church member and her father said to her, "Con, I hope you'll vote for keeping separate."

Although Mum was grown up and was now a trained teacher she daren't go against her father. She abstained, although she believed in union!

1

Harry worked for a shoe firm in Kettering and when he got married his boss called him into his office.

"I hear you've got a wife now, Harry. I'll raise your wages by a shilling a week"!

The wife was Mary Cherry (better known as Polly) a devout, serious and godly girl. Harry rose to become manager in the firm. Later he left the shoe business and bought his own grocery shop in Luton.

When they retired Harry and Polly went to live in a village near Bedford. Polly led the Women's Meeting in the Methodist Church. She had a hundred women in her group and showed real pastoral care for each one. She never let her 'left hand know what her right hand was doing' and would bake a cake for one, take a few eggs to another, shop for a sick friend or iron for another; but she never gossiped or passed on tales. My mother always referred to her as "a very good woman".

Grandad died just short of his 96th birthday. He woke up that day sensing that he would die not because he was ill but because it was his time to die. All that day he kept saying, "I'm going home today, going home to glory!" He died in the evening.

My own mother, Connie, was of the same calibre as her mother. At the age of 12 she committed her life to Jesus. She was the middle of three daughters – Elsie was five years older and Gladys five years younger. Only Connie went on to higher education, winning a scholarship to Bedford Grammar School for Girls. She cycled every day to the station in Kettering where they lived and left her bike at the station where she collected it on her return. After Bedford she went to Homerton College in Cambridge and trained to be a teacher. She taught for seven years at the Bath Road School in Kettering where she had attended as a girl.

Connie was brought up as a Methodist and attended the various meetings and functions. She had a lovely natural contralto voice and sang in the choir. She was often in the chapel concerts. She played the piano well and was a good accompanist.

The Rudland side of my family were very different from the Middletons. Great-grandfather Rudland, who was born in Monkwearmouth, Sunderland, went to France and Italy to learn to paint. He was attracted to the Italian style of painting and when he returned to England he adopted the title of 'Signor'. He altered 'Rudland' to the more romantic sounding name 'Durland' and became known thereafter as 'Signor Durland'. He set up in Birmingham as a portrait painter. Portraits didn't pay well, however, and he found he could earn more painting scenery for the theatre. This introduced him to the world of entertainment. He ran a circus in Birmingham and later returned to the town of his birth. In Sunderland he opened his own theatre, 'The Star Music Hall'. One can read about his variety shows from the newspapers of the day – famous dancers, singers, acrobats and even boxers.

Signor Durland prospered in his new career and became a well-known character in the town. He made money and was generous with it. Legend has it that he threw money to the poor from his landau and received a letter from Queen Victoria thanking him for his various acts of generosity. He showed a real concern for the plight of the miners and supported their newly formed union, offering the use of his theatre for their meetings. He also organised soup kitchens.

Tragedy struck on the evening of Saturday 16th August 1888. One of the features of the theatre was the central light in the ceiling. There were seventy gas jets giving a brilliant light. As a signal for the start of the show the pressure on the central gas jets was increased and then reduced. It was very effective in raising the expectation of the theatregoers. However, over the years the ceiling timbers dried out as a result of the heat from the central light. When the pressure was increased on August 16th it ignited the timbers and fire spread rapidly. There was a packed house of about 1,000 people. There was only one exit from the gallery and a panic stampede could lead to injury and loss of life. Signor Durland spoke from the stage. His charismatic presence and clear voice controlled the audience.

3

"Please leave quietly. Everything is under control." They made their way from the gallery to the one exit in an orderly fashion. No one panicked. All got out safely; but the theatre was in a sorry state. Half the theatre was gutted. The newly painted scenery and props were destroyed. The theatre was rebuilt and struggled on for a few years, but it could not be freed from the heavy debts caused by the fire. His fellow citizens felt for him. Mr. Wilson, later MP for Sunderland, organised a couple of concerts for him, but he had to let go of the Star Music Hall.

Signor Durland travelled from place to place with various shows and returned to Sunderland with his 'Egyptian Hall of Mysteries'. He was a distinguished figure with his white hair and beard and his Stetson hat in the style of Buffalo Bill. He was an enterprising and generous man, larger than life and with a tremendous personality.

My great-grandfather married Sarah and they had three children – Louise who became an actress starring in Victorian melodrama, William who helped to stage manage the shows and later became a money lender and Fred, my grandfather. Fred followed in his father's footsteps and became a circus owner, fairground proprietor and travelling showman. He was known as 'The Great Durlando, the illusionist'. Fred married Annie Gardener from Birmingham whose father was a gunsmith. With Annie and his ever growing family he travelled from city to city – Birmingham, Liverpool, Leeds, London, Newcastle, Edinburgh. I can trace the itinerary from the cities where the children were born!

All the family spent some time involved in the fairground or circus. Aunt Beatie remembered riding on elephants. My Dad was the head of the human spider! Grandma was 'Madame Durland' the fortune teller. In 1902 the family reached Edinburgh and Annie had had enough of the travelling life. She settled in Edinburgh. She found rooms to let and kept one room for her fortune telling clientele. She did the only thing she knew to care for her family. Fred, however, continued travelling and took his favourite son with him – Dick, my father.

Fred was a typical Rudland, ingenious and enterprising. When he ran the circus he had a troupe of black men whom he advertised as being primitive savages. They would come into the ring with Annie apparently in charge of them. Less than five feet tall, she would have a whip in her hand and a bandage on her wrist but would exercise amazing control of these vicious savages! One day they went whooping and shouting into a butcher's shop. They grabbed whatever they could – shoulders of lamb, legs of pork, sausages – and raced down the street hungrily eating the raw meat! Of course they were arrested and had to appear before the Magistrate. The Great Durlando spoke on their behalf and was abject in his apologies. "I'm very sorry. They are but ignorant savages. They don't understand English so I must speak on their behalf. I give my full assurance that this will not happen again." It was, of course, all a publicity stunt and the resulting publicity brought in the crowds. I understand this happened in a number of cities!

When Fred and his son Dick were travelling they sometimes had plenty of money, and Fred would give his son more money than he knew how to handle. Other times they had nothing and ate even the leaves from the hawthorn hedges. Soon Dick had had enough. Fred was drinking more and more and when drunk he treated his workers with contempt. They hated him and several times tried to kill him. His young son had to be on constant lookout and saved his father on a number of occasions. One day, when he was twelve, father and son reached Dunbar. It must have been a flush period, for Dick had some money. A boat was leaving for Leith, the port of Edinburgh. Dick paid his fare and went home to Mum. At last a settled home and the opportunity of going to school.

Dick had little education during his travelling days, but he was intelligent and quick to learn. In his teenage years he became a Christian and as such felt that it was wrong to fight. The Great War came and he was called up. He appeared before a tribunal because of his beliefs. He was accused of being a coward.

"No sir," he replied. "I'm no coward. You can send me to the

front line if you want but I won't take a gun."

They took him at his word. He was sent to the front line in France where he was wounded. His case came up in Parliament and they declared that he should never have been sent to the front line. When he recovered from his wounds he was sent back to England and transferred to the Non Combatant Corps. He was given the job of breaking in and training horses.

His work with horses brought him to Kettering. He and some other Christians in the camp went one Sunday evening to worship at Bath Street Methodist Church. As the service was about to start, the choir filed in. Among the contraltos was a beautiful young lady with long chestnut hair. Immediately Dick felt he would like to hold her within his coat. The girl bowed her head, prayed and then looked down on the congregation. Her eyes were immediately drawn to the handsome young soldier with dark wavy hair and Italian-like features. She felt she would like to snuggle inside his coat!

After the Service a white-haired gentleman asked the young soldiers if they would like to come to his home for supper. They agreed. As Dick sat at the table he saw sitting opposite him the young contralto! She was Connie, the daughter of the white haired Harry Middleton. The two started going out together. After the war they got married. Academically they seemed unsuited. She was well educated and a teacher. Dick had hardly any formal education, had no job, no training except to break in horses! Her mother asked Connie if she was sure she was doing the right thing. "I've prayed about it," she answered, "and I feel it's what God wants." It was truly a love match. It had been love at first sight!

2

"If there is a God, show yourself to me."

Dad sat in the waiting room of Elsie Inglis Maternity Home in Edinburgh waiting for the news of his first child. Would it be a boy or a girl? Would Con be all right? He had insisted that she have the very best care. The Maternity Home was expensive but he loved her so much, what did money matter? They had waited four years for this moment. How they had longed for a child! The door opened. "Mr Rudland, you have a baby daughter!" Eagerly Dick rose from his seat and followed the nurse to where Con lay, exhausted but happy.

"Chip," he murmured, using his favourite name for her as he kissed her tenderly. He walked over to the cot and instinctively bent over to pick up the baby.

"I'm sorry," the nurse said. "You can't pick your baby up. She has a broken leg."

"Broken? What do you mean?" he asked, hardly able to believe his ears.

"The birth was difficult," the nurse replied. "She was born breach and the cord was wrapped twice around her neck. It wasn't easy for the doctor."

"What are you doing about it?" Dad asked.

"We're just leaving it," the nurse replied. "It will heal on its own. It will be all right."

It was not all right. Every time she bathed me Mum cried. At first the leg hung limp and then the two parts linked but were overlapping. She thought I would have one leg shorter than the

other. The cord around my neck had nearly strangled me. As it was it caused an umbilical hernia which had to be repaired later in my life. But the most worrying thing was the nasty growth on my back. As I grew, so it grew too, not only outwards but inwards and was affecting my internal organs.

Mum and Dad prayed fervently for their little daughter and God answered their prayers. When the leg was X-rayed later, the overlapping bones were found to have slipped back into place! The growth in my back, however, continued to grow. It was probably cancerous. When I was sixteen months old it was decided that I should undergo surgery to have it removed. The cut was diagonally from my shoulder to my waist. It needed twenty-two stitches. An ugly scar I was to carry for the rest of my life. But worse was to come. Somehow or other the operation caused meningitis to affect my spine. I went into a deep coma. The doctors told Mum and Dad I would die. There was no cure for meningitis at that time. They wanted me to stay in hospital.

"If that's all you can promise then we shall keep her at home," was my parents' response. They wrote to all their Christian friends. "Please pray for our little Glady. The doctors say she will die."

Dad had to continue going to work but Mum kept a constant vigil by my side. She was pregnant with my brother. I don't think she slept properly as day after day and night after night she sat praying for a miracle. Suddenly, after a fortnight in the coma, I opened my eyes!

"Pam," I said. I was just beginning to talk and 'pam' meant 'pram'. I was asking to go out in the pram! Mum was overjoyed. She rang the doctor.

"Glady has regained consciousness and is asking to go out. Can I take her?"

"Yes," said the doctor, "but only for a few minutes."

Mum wrapped me well and took me out and I caught whooping cough! But I had come through!

I was very weak and vulnerable. I went from one infection to another, catching all the childhood illnesses including scarlet fever, rheumatism and anaemia. At one stage I had a calliper on my leg. Was it to correct a wobbly walk? Later it was found that I had shallow hips and in later life I needed complete hip replacements. Was it to correct my toes? The extreme weakness I experienced was causing me to claw my toes, a common feature in children trying to walk after severe illness. After my coma my parents had to teach me to walk again.

Although I was often ill I was happy. I knew Mum and Dad loved me and I had a little brother, David, not much younger than myself and we were great pals. Mum treated us more or less like twins. We had matching coats with hat or cap in the same material. If there was a special cake it was cut in two and we each had a half. We played together very happily, usually in creative ways. On a Saturday morning we played on Mum and Dad's big bed and it became a ship, or a house or whatever we fancied. We had a great many stuffed toys and dolls, and we played with these imaginatively. Once we built a theatre; half the dolls were actors, the others the audience. We dressed up the actors and made tickets for the ticket office.

We had "school" every day. I took the older "children" and David the "younger ones". Sometimes we played "church", my teddy being the preacher. One day we had a wedding and David's teddy "Bimsy" married my doll "Doreen". They were given the spare room as their home and Bimsy asked "Big Mummy" (my mother) for a job "now that I'm a married man!" He became the house dustman. He had a stuffed animal for his horse and a little cart in which he put sweet papers or any other bits of rubbish he found. He was given a penny a week! At Christmas we hung up a large stocking for my dolls and a large stocking for David's. On Christmas morning we were so excited about this that we looked at the dolls' stockings before our own! We both had the same idea and gave Bimsy and Doreen a little teddy so they ended up with twins! When my cousin Charlie came to

9

stay at New Year we dressed the dolls up as explorers. The snow lay thick in our back garden and the dolls set off to discover the North Pole.

Charlie was staying with us because at Christmas and New Year we had great family celebrations. On Christmas Day we all went to Grandma's house. She lived with my three aunts – Louie, Lena and Lily. Next door lived Aunt Beatie and Uncle Charlie with their four sons. We would all stay the night and next day went to Aunt Beatie's. For New Year they would all come to us and stay the night. We all had big houses. At each house we would have a party and the Rudland parties were great. Being a theatrical family they were skilled at entertaining. The charades were hilarious. I'll never forget the shadow acting behind a sheet when Uncle Charlie, the "surgeon", operated on Aunt Lena, the "patient", and took from her extended stomach (a balloon which had to be "cut") sausages and all manner of things. It was all very real to my young eyes.

My cousins were very musical and they would play for us – violin and piano. I went to elocution lessons so I would recite some poems. Dad did all kinds of tricks, some of which he had learned in the fairground. Aunt Lena would sing.

Under our house were some cellars and one in particular had never been explored by us. One day David, his friend Fred and I decided we would find out where it led. We started off with a candle. After a while we found there was a break in the floor that was quite deep and wide. We were just working out how to get across when Fred blew out the candle and screamed. We all rushed back to the entrance, never to explore the secrets of that cellar. Despite all the sickness and sadness of my early years I had a very happy childhood.

When I was about eight I had had so much illness and become so weak that I could no longer eat. The doctor made an appointment for me to see a specialist at the Sick Children's Hospital. Mum took me by bus and we started to walk up the long avenue leading to the hospital. Before very long it was obvious I could not make the journey and Mum had to carry me. As I stood before the specialist I collapsed and it was decided that I should stay in the hospital. I was suffering from debility and they tried to get me to eat. I was there for a month, getting weaker all the time. They could do nothing for me. My three aunts who stayed with Grandma said, "Send Glady to us". For a month I stayed with them. I was pampered, praised, fussed over and given tit-bits of anything I fancied. I grew stronger and went home well – but vain and spoilt! However, the rough and tumble of family life soon knocked that out of me!

There was a new baby at home: little Harry, and Mum needed help. Our large Victorian house had four storeys and we let out some of the rooms. Mum had a girl who lived in and helped with some of the chores. We all loved little Harry, a gurgling laughing baby. I remember a happy holiday spent in North Berwick when I was eight. I felt well for once, except for nits in my hair which we all picked up from school in those days.

Sadly, our happiness with Harry was short lived. When he was 20 months old he developed pneumonia. Unfortunately he was wrongly diagnosed by the doctor, and by the time another doctor was called in it was too late. I remember very clearly the day Harry died. I came skipping home from school and arrived to find that Harry had just died. He lay on the bed my parents had had brought down to the sitting room for him. Mum quickly sent for Dad. When he came in he dropped to the floor on his knees beside the bed and said, "Harry, speak to me." There was, of course, no answer. "Oh, there is no God," was my father's anguished cry as he broke down, sobbing uncontrollably.

"No God"! The statement shocked me. No God! But Mum and Dad had always told me there was a God. Dad had faced death because he believed there was a God! I had accepted it as children accept there is a Santa Claus, or fairies at the bottom of the garden. No God! I had to find the truth about God's existence not so much for my sake but for Dad's. His grief was all-consuming. He locked himself in the room with the little body of his dear son. When they

11

finally took Harry away (how well I remember him in his little white coffin) Dad could not bring himself to leave the grave. When the time came to lock the gates they had to force Dad to leave the cemetery. After they dragged him from the grave he just kept walking round and round the cemetery walls. I don't think he ever fully got over his grief. Both he and Mum were trapped into a pit of grief. It was only when a neighbour pointed out that David and I were being neglected that they began to take notice of us again; but the scars of grief ran deep.

I felt I had a task to do! I had to find out whether or not there was a God. The cemetery was just down the road from our house. After school I would sit by Harry's grave.

"Oh God," I prayed, "if there is a God, show Yourself to me. Is there a Heaven and is Harry there?"

Day after day and week after week I kept this prayer vigil until one day there was born in my spirit an assurance that there was a God, there was a Heaven and Harry was there. That day I went home with a lighter step.

"Daddy," I said, "there is a God."

Later Mum told me that that did more than anything else to bring back my father's faith.

There was still the awful void where Harry had been and my parents decided to have another child to take his place. Mum was forty-four by this time. A boy, Dickie, was born. He had Down's Syndrome. Dickie was a happy child as such babies often are, but he was very slow to learn. He was five years old before he learned to use the toilet. He never learned to read or write and only spoke a few words pronounced like an eighteen-month-old child. I was 'Giga', David was 'Did-did'. Only Mummy and Daddy were said in an understandable way. Mum and Dad loved their little handicapped son. In those days such children were usually hidden away but Mum and Dad never did so with Dickie. Dad had to swallow his pride as he introduced Dickie to people, but he never hid him away. Mum had most to do with Dickie and her patience was tried to the limit; but her love never wavered.

The grief of having a Down's Syndrome child followed quickly upon the grief of losing Harry. David and I watched with bewilderment as our parents struggled yet again with sorrow. We had to do something!

One day we sat on the stairs talking it over. We loved Dickie but we loved our parents more. "If only he wasn't there, they'd be happy again," we stated simplistically. Then the idea came – we could kill him! We stated this with no emotion, simply as a fact. We'd be put in prison but Mum and Dad would be happy again. The foolishness of children! But it was our way, in our ignorance, of trying to solve the problem. Of course, fortunately the idea never took root, but it showed how deeply children can feel their parents' emotions and try to do something to help.

This was a passing thought. The main thing was that I now knew there was a God. I resolved to get to know Him. Mum and Dad had not insisted that we attend Sunday School. The choice was left to us. David never attended but I did. I also went to the Methodist Church with my mother. I remember asking her one day if I could take communion. She asked the church leaders and they agreed it would be all right. I never asked again but it was very meaningful to me. I felt I wanted a girl of my own age to go with me to church, so I invited my special friend to go with me to the local Presbyterian Church. She came once or twice but was not really interested, so I looked for someone who was. There was a girl in my class who regularly went to church, so I asked her if I could go with her. She was pleased I had asked her and the next Sunday, dressed in my new green fitted coat and Deanna Durbin hat, I set out to find her church. It was quite a long way from our house and when I got there I found she was in the choir. I was invited to participate, and this I did, joining her in worship every Sunday. It was my introduction to a Baptist Church.

One day Dad told us that he had been chosen to train in Glasgow to become a manager with his firm, the Brooke Bond company. This meant that Dad was away during every week and only came home at weekends. David and I always met him at the railway station and he always took us for a milkshake. The war had started and Dad was in the long Glasgow air raid. The window in his room crashed in with the blast and it was only the drawn curtain that saved his life.

When Dad finished his training he was made the Group Manager for the North of England based in Leeds. He only had the Directors above him, which is a remarkable achievement for the boy who had had so little schooling. A house was found for us and very quickly we had to move. The house was very different from our four storey Victorian house in Edinburgh. It was a white, flat-roofed semi and seemed very modern and continental. Leeds meant very little to me. I knew Dad had been born there. I knew it was an important railway junction on the way to the Midlands where we had spent holidays with grandparents and an aunt, but little more. Leeds was now our home. What lay in store? It was as if I had been uprooted from 'Bonnie Scotland' and planted in an unknown place. I had just turned fourteen.

3

"You ought to start preaching"

$\mathbf{A}$ new school was found for David and me – West Leeds High School. We had to travel on two trams, one into the centre of Leeds and the other out to West Leeds. We got lost the first day and were too late to sit the entrance exam. We were asked what we had done at school previously. I was advanced in most subjects and they were going to put me in a class above my year, the lower fifth, until they asked what English History I had done.

"Only as it pertained to the Scottish," I answered in true Scottish manner. They put me in the upper fourth. In the playground the girls gathered round me.

"Say something," they requested.

"I dinnie ken whit to say," I answered.

"That's right. Say something else."

I was a born mimic, however, and was soon talking Yorkshire like the rest of them.

The school was in two halves – boys and girls in separate classes. We shared a common hall with assemblies at different times. We had one activity together – the joint choir. We met after school on Fridays and it was the highlight of the week. We sang such works as Handel's Messiah, Hiawatha's Wedding Feast and Haydn's Creation.

I was popular at school with both pupils and staff, and in my final year, the upper sixth, I was made Head Girl. We had a new Headmistress, Miss Guest, and she called me into her room at the beginning of the year.

"Gladys," she said, "I'm going to put the discipline of the school into the hands of yourself and the prefects."

We felt very honoured but also very conscious of the power handed to us. If a girl did something wrong she was called before the prefects. We sat at a long table in the library, our form room. I sat at the head of the table with the wrongdoer's house captain on my left. The prefects were ranged down the sides of the table. "What has this girl done?" I would be asked. And we would all be suitably horrified at the answer. We would give her some punishment such as lines to copy or a poem to learn.

We found the girls were more afraid of us than they were of the teachers! As Head Girl I was chosen to represent the school at a conference in Edinburgh. My friend Doreen went with me. It was a good time and broadened our experience as we met young people from all over the country. It was also my responsibility to give the speech on behalf of the girls at Speech Day. I entered for the annual Shakespeare Speech Competition and won every year. I had a choice for my prizes and always chose the complete works of one of the classical poets.

Life was good. Many people hate their teenage years when they are neither adult nor child, but I loved it. I could choose – playing games one day and 'dressing up' and going out the next. I didn't feel an 'awkward in-between'. I felt I was either and both, a child and an adult. And I felt well! All the weaknesses and illnesses of my childhood were gone. Having had so many diseases it was as if I had built up an immunity and I don't remember being ill during my teenage years. It was as if Life came and held out his hands and said, "Come, run with me", and I ran! I romped through those years, glad to be alive.

It was the Spring following our move to Leeds and I was reading my Bible. I had found a church, continuing my search for God who I knew existed but I didn't yet know personally. I had joined the Chapel Allerton Methodist Young People's Fellowship which met on

Sunday afternoons. I had also joined Girls' League, a missionary organisation, and the Methodist Group Fellowship. I was introduced to the last two by Annie Best, a Local Preacher who took me under her wing. She gave me Bible reading notes and taught me how to have a daily Quiet Time. So here I was in my room with the sunshine streaming through my window. As I read my Bible I came to the words in Romans 6:23: "The wages of sin is death". I didn't understand what this meant but the words stood out of the page. I knew the words were important, so I reflected on them. There was no one to ask but I believe the Holy Spirit was there waiting to minister to my seeking heart. I saw that we all die not because of illness or accident but because of sin making our bodies mortal. But then why did Jesus die? He was sinless. It wouldn't be the Cross that did it – I'd already ruled that out. Then I saw it. It was sin! But not His. It was mine! I could do no other than give my life to Him who had died for me. Suddenly, God became personal to me. He had come to me in Jesus.

Eagerly I looked forward each day to reading my Bible, for there I was finding God as He spoke to me through His Word. I didn't know that other people knew Him in the way I had discovered. The church I attended was not evangelical and personal religion was not taught. How I longed to have fellowship with others. As I read on in my Bible I found that Paul knew Jesus in this personal way and I began to have fellowship with him! How ignorant I was! I knew Jesus and Paul knew Jesus but I didn't know any others who did! That Summer I went to my first Christian Conference. It was a simple affair where we packed palliasses with hay and slept in a church hall. I found other people talking of knowing Jesus personally, and for the first time I began to have fellowship with other Christians. How precious it was to me.

I was never a 'pretty' girl but I began to find that boys were attracted to me. I suppose growing up with my brother and meeting his friends I was used to talking with boys and had an easy manner

with them. My first boyfriend was Ken from church. He wanted to 'go all the way' and I wasn't willing, so after a few dates, he left me for his 'cousin'. Then there was Len, the boy next door. He, Jean who lived opposite, my brother David and I formed a foursome. We played together, board and card games in the winter and cycling in the summer. Near where we lived there was a large piece of land we called "the dump" and there we played cowboys and Indians using our bikes as horses. Sometimes we cycled to places like Adel or Harewood. There were times when I went out alone with Len to the theatre or cinema or to a dance. Len wanted to marry me but I knew he was not the one for me.

The war was still on and if there was an air raid during the night we would all meet in the middle of the street in darkness because of the blackout. Unable to see each other we said, "It's a fraud, Claude." "It's a swizzle, Cecil" was the answer. If the raid went on beyond 2.00 a.m. we could arrive at school later than usual. In our childish way, of course, we hoped it would!

Leeds was full of soldiers – American, Canadian, Polish as well as British. A friend and I, as girls have done from time immemorial, sometimes went into town on a Saturday evening to 'pick up' a boy. It was just a sort of game to us. One night we were taken by two Canadian boys to their camp and given fried eggs and bacon! Of course the boys we met wanted to have sex, but although I was a flirt I knew as a Christian that that was not right. Although I had many boyfriends I remained a virgin till I married. I never saw any danger in this flirting. Looking back I believe God protected me. I saw no wrong in flirting and sometimes found opportunity to witness to the boys. It all seemed quite consistent with my Christian commitment. I would be fifteen or sixteen.

My parents were quite liberal in the way I was brought up and allowed my brother and me to go on holiday without them. When I was fifteen and David was only thirteen we went youth hostelling and cycled to the Peak District. The next year we cycled to North Wales. These were great adventures. We pre-booked the hostels but we had

to follow the map to find our way on unknown roads. It helped to develop our independence and sense of self-reliance.

When I was seventeen my Minister, the Rev Dr Percy Scott said, "Gladys, you ought to start preaching." As soon as he said it I remembered an incident when I was a child. I always wanted to be an actress, an artist and a poet. I suppose it was in my blood. Mum belonged to a dramatic society and I wanted to join, but the producer said I was too young. I would have to wait until I was fourteen. She suggested that I should have elocution lessons with her to prepare for joining the group. She was a Roman Catholic and taught me religious poems as well as children's verse. My Aunt Louie belonged to a Christian choir and often sang solo parts. Sometimes she took me to the meetings they led and I would recite a devotional poem.

One day we went to a Mission Hall in the High Street in Edinburgh. After the meeting an old lady in black shawl came and thanked us. "The meeting has blessed me," she said. "Thank you". I was touched! So one could sing. Or preach or recite and it blessed people! "One day, when I'm grown up, I'll preach for Jesus," I vowed. Now I was being asked to consider this very thing! It seemed God had spoken to me.

"Yes," I said to Dr Scott. "Yes, I will if you'll help me." I jumped on my bike, raced home and ran inside.

"Mummy, I'm going to preach for Jesus!"

Dr Scott was a great help to me. He later became the Principal of the Methodist College in Manchester. Instead of doing the studies by correspondence he taught me himself. I well remember when I sat in his study for my first lesson.

"What is faith?" he asked.

"Faith is, well it's er, it's ..."

"Come on. You'll have to do better than that if you're going to preach," he said. "And because you're a woman, you'll have to do better than men!"

Soon I was off to Teacher Training College with my close school

friend Doreen. I was accepted at the College of my choice – St Katherine's, Liverpool. Although the war was over the College was still evacuated to Keswick in the Lake District. The College virtually took over the town. The Queen's Hotel in the town centre was our headquarters. We lived in various guest houses, had P.E. in the Drill Hall, assembly in the cinema and lectures in various church halls. We had English on a Wednesday morning in a large house across Derwentwater. We got there by minibus but returned by boat! It was all great fun.

The scenery was breathtaking. I fell in love with nature in the Lake District, for it was the first time I had lived in the countryside. In the notorious winter of 1947 Doreen and I went youth hostelling at half term. The mountains were snow covered, icicles three feet long hung from the rocks and the lakes were frozen. We wondered why sometimes we were the only ones in the hostels!

Doreen lived at some distance from the town centre. She had to walk through a wood to reach where she was staying so I used to walk with her and return on my own. One day when I was walking back I met a man who was well known as someone to be avoided by the girls. What should I do? As he approached me I gave a quick prayer and decided to show no fear and treat him as I would any other person. We chatted as we walked and I even allowed him to take my arm but nothing else happened. When I got to my boarding house I told the girls I had met him. "What did you do?" they asked in horror. I told them and they were amazed. Once again God had protected me.

After eighteen months we went back to the College in Liverpool, so I had the privilege of enjoying both sides of college life. Because I was on the College Council I was given an end room which was larger than the others. This was useful for prayer meetings, as I was President of the Christian Union. At first the Principal would not allow us to meet because we offered extempore prayer, so we met where we could outside. A priest, Father Cox, was sent to the College and the Principal put all spiritual matters into his hands. It was arranged that I should meet Father Cox and discuss the matter of the prayer meetings. The C.U. prayed as I asked Father Cox if the group could hold prayer meetings in my room. I returned to the group with the desired answer to their prayers: we had permission for our prayer meetings!

While I was at College I continued my studies for lay preaching, and began to feel a call to full-time ministry. I shared this with Dr Scott after I came home and started teaching. In those days the Methodist Church only ordained men to the full-time ministry. He suggested that I might apply to the Baptist or Congregational Churches who did ordain women.

"I could never be anything but a Methodist," I said in my youthful arrogance.

"What about the Deaconess Order?" he suggested.

So I went to the Deaconess College in Ilkley to look round and to discuss the issue. I came away knowing that it was the ordained ministry I was called to. That summer the Methodist Conference debated the issue of ordaining women. I was, of course, very interested in the outcome and felt that in a very real sense they were debating my future! They decided that the ordination of women was all right in principle but that it was not right, at the time, to put it into practice! I felt personally rejected; but I knew God had called me and it was over to Him how this was to be worked out.

4

"You ought to get on well together"

"Will you come over for tea next Sunday?" asked Doreen. "After tea we can go to church together."

We were both now teaching in Leeds. Doreen lived over on the York Road side and I on the Harrogate Road and so we went to different churches. Quite often we went to each other's homes and churches but this day was to prove different.

After the service one of the young people said to us, "Come back to our place for supper and we can have a sing-song round the piano."

Quite a number of us made our way to his house. As we walked he introduced me to a young man I'd not seen before.

"Jock, meet Glady. You ought to get on well together; you both come from Edinburgh."

And so we quizzed each other. "Where did you live?" "What school did you go to? ..."

That night Dennis, who had introduced us, played Debussy's "Clair de Lune" on the piano. We never forgot that piece of music and it became a kind of symbol of our meeting. Over the next few weeks I met Jock on a number of occasions when the young people met for various functions. One of these was a social on St Valentine's Day. There was a game where we needed to write down some answers and I didn't have anything to write with. All the other young people seemed to be in groups or pairs. Jock, who was very much a newcomer, stood on his own.

"Have you got a pencil?" I asked. He had and we paired up for the evening. That question, like the music, became a kind of symbol!

One evening I had tonsillitis and couldn't go to the young people's gathering. Doreen was telling me what happened and mentioned, "Bill was there."

"Bill? Who's he?" I asked.

"Jock," she answered. "His real name is Bill."

Immediately I was interested! I was beginning to be attracted to this shy blue-eyed young Scot.

As a group a number of the young people started going dancing at the nearby Temple Newsam Golf Club.

The first night we went neither Bill nor I had a partner. I knew Bill was too shy to ask me, so I said to him, "Shall we dance?"

"I might ruin your nylons," he answered.

However, we did dance together, and from then on we nearly always danced together – waltz, quickstep, slow foxtrot. Two of the favourite tunes were "Buttons and Bows" and "Twelfth Street Rag". Gradually, we were falling in love.

Bill asked me to go to the cinema with him. We saw "The Passionate Friends". Then I invited him to tea one Sunday and he met the family. I remember him sitting on the floor playing with Dickie. In the afternoon we walked through the nearby woods. No cuddling, no kissing – we just talked, getting to know each other. We went to church that night and Bill came back to supper. I went to the gate to bid him goodnight and he kissed me – just a little peck – but as I went in I was conscious that my cheeks were burning and stars were in my eyes.

Soon after that I attended a Methodist Group Fellowship Conference in Bournemouth. From there I wrote to Bill and told him what was happening at the meetings. Then I asked him, "Do you love Jesus like I do?"

The next time we went out together I asked him what he thought about my question. I told him about people at the conference who'd received Jesus.

He said, "I wish I could go to a conference, then I could become a Christian too."

I told him he didn't need to go to a conference. He could receive Jesus anywhere, even here – we were in Temple Newsam Park. And there, among the rhododendrons Bill made his commitment to Jesus; not because I had asked him but because Jesus had been drawing him gradually over the years. As a child in Edinburgh he had wished that someone would ask him to Sunday School, but no one ever did. When he was evacuated in the war he was cared for by a lovely Christian lady in St Andrews who taught him the Lord's Prayer and took him to church. One night, he and some other apprentices had wandered into the Halton Methodist Church Youth Club. He was attracted to the Christians there and started going to church. Now, this was the first time that Christ had been offered to him and he was ready to receive.

I gave Bill a Bible for his birthday and he was hungry to learn about God. Within six months he knew as much as I did. Our knowledge of God grew as we shared together. Our love grew too and I felt so unworthy of him. He had kept himself for the right girl and he hadn't even been a Christian! I had been brought up in a Christian home and had been committed to Christ for six years yet I had lost count of the number of boys I had kissed. My lips felt dirty and felt unworthy of his embrace. I told him about the others. He said it didn't matter. I asked for his forgiveness, which he readily gave. I felt I could start all over again.

Our relationship developed quickly. We had met in the January and in the July Bill asked me to marry him. I told him I wanted to but had thought several times in the past that I had met the right one.

"I want to be sure," I said. "I want God's choice."

"So do I," Bill said, and we wondered what to do.

My Aunt Louie was staying with us enjoying a holiday. She had always been a spiritual help to me, so I turned to her.

24

"How shall we find God's will?"

"Put aside some months," she said, "and ask God for His answer."

I told Bill what she had said and we agreed on a plan. We would go on seeing each other but just as friends. After five months we would share together what we felt God had said. During this time we would not seek to influence each other. Only after the five months would we share how we had each been led.

I got my answer very quickly. In the August I again went to a conference in Reading. A girl was asked to share her testimony. She was physically handicapped and had not had much education. Why should she be asked, I thought, instead of me? I was well educated and could express myself better. What pride! What sin! When I heard her testimony I was wounded to the core. I felt I had to get away somewhere on my own. Burning tears of shame coursed down my cheeks. "Forgive me!" I cried. "Oh Lord, forgive me."

I was sitting on a fallen tree trunk at the bottom of the conference centre grounds. As always happens when we truly cry to the Lord, He answered. He came to me in His mercy and grace and forgave me. He dried my tears and as I sat there with a new consciousness of His Presence, I suddenly knew God wanted me to marry Bill. It was as if in that new clean forgiven moment with no barrier between me and my Lord I could plainly see His will for me. I knew then that it included marriage to Bill. I have never doubted it ever since. But I would have to keep this to myself until after Christmas.

Bill didn't get his answer until December. He was praying one day and as he prayed he had a vision. He had never had such an experience before and it was totally unexpected. As he was praying he saw a series of 'still pictures', much like a slide show. He saw Jesus on the Cross, but at some distance. Next he saw me at the foot of the Cross. The next 'still' he saw us both kneeling at the foot of the Cross. Then he saw the view looking up into the face of Jesus. This was followed by the only movement in this set of 'still pictures'.

25

Jesus, looking down at us both as we knelt, nodded His head in a way that said "Yes". As Bill pondered what all this meant he realised that Jesus was saying that it was His will for us to get married.

After Christmas we met to share our answers. We sat either side of the fireplace and told each other our experiences. As soon as we knew the answer we sprang into each other's arms! We were now engaged! Bill could now fully understand the significance of the 'pictures' he had seen. I was at the foot of the Cross and had received my answer there (my experience at Reading) and, as he came to the Cross, Jesus could now reveal His will to him.

We planned a party to tell our friends. We decided not to tell them about our engagement until the actual party where we would exchange rings. I bought a special dress for the occasion. Bill's favourite colour was blue, so I bought a blue taffeta dress with a wide collar and full skirt. Together we bought the rings. Mine was a diamond ring with three diamonds set in hearts. The middle heart was bigger than the other two and we saw this as representing God who joined the two lesser hearts, Bill and myself. Bill's ring was a simple signet ring.

What was Bill's background? He was one of a large family of seven children. His father was born in the island of Burray in Orkney. Bill has traced his family tree and the Rosie family goes back for centuries. They originated in Mainland, the largest of the Orkney Islands, and then moved to the small island of Burray and later to South Ronaldsay. Orkney is a delightful place and not as cold as one might think, as the warm Gulf Stream blesses its shores. The winter nights are long and the days short. The lovely long days of summer mean that it hardly gets dark and it is possible to read out of doors at midnight! The traditional way of life is that the people have smallholdings and they fish the fruitful seas. They are referred to as fishermen with ploughs. Orkney belonged to Norway until the fifteenth century when the King of Norway gave the islands to Scotland as a dowry for his daughter Margaret who married King

James the Third of Scotland.

The people of Orkney don't consider themselves as Scots. Their blood is Viking. They have no clans or tartans and proudly refer to themselves as Orcadians. People have lived in Orkney since the Stone Age. You can visit Skara Brae, a village built 5,000 years ago! There are ancient stone circles and burial mounds that are older than the Pyramids. Like all Orcadian men, Bill's Dad, Sandy Rosie, could turn his hand to anything. Sadly, Sandy's mother died in giving birth to him and when he was four his father remarried. Sandy was brought up by a very loving stepmother. When he was 18 he was called up into the Royal Navy in 1917. After two years in the navy he became a merchant seaman.

Once when he was ashore and visiting Edinburgh he met Maggie Scott, a weaver who had moved from Hawick to work in one of the woollen mills in Edinburgh. They set up home in Edinburgh. It was a very happy marriage, but after some years Sandy's health broke. A measles epidemic struck many in Edinburgh. Sandy and Maggie had three children and the youngest – 18 month old John – died. Sandy almost died due to the measles. He was no longer able to go to sea. He lost two stones in weight, which he never recovered; his hands shook and his hearing became permanently impaired. It was difficult to get work during the 1930s, but Sandy did bricklaying, made furniture and even taught himself to make kilts! Maggie was a born entertainer and had a good voice. She often sang at various gatherings. She was known in the local community as Ma Rosie and was called in to deliver the babies.

There was interesting repetition of history. When Sandy was 12 the local school in Burray recognised that he was bright and they wanted him to go to the Grammar School in Kirkwall. This would have meant staying in Kirkwall during the week and only coming home at weekends. The family was too poor for this to happen since they needed his help. A compromise was reached. With some others, Sandy was given two further years at school in Burray and so was able to help with the family smallholding and the fishing.

Bill, however, was more fortunate. When he was was 15 (the school-leaving age) he was the dux (top) of the school and his parents were approached about his going to Leith Academy for a further two years to get his 'Highers'. They agreed that he should do so. A bursary grant was made available to help out with the finances. No doubt Sandy's missed opportunity had something to do with their decision. Getting his Highers was to prove vital for the later qualifications for engineering and the ministry.

Bill's family didn't go to church, but as a child Bill longed to go to Sunday School. When war broke out, Bill with his older brother Alex and younger sister Ella, was evacuated, along with many other children, to St Andrews. On arrival in that beautiful town by the sea, the large group was gathered in a school hall. Local people came and chose the children they were willing to house. Alex, Bill and Ella determined that they would not be separated, but not many wanted to take on three children from central Edinburgh. When nearly all the children had found homes a silver-haired lady entered the hall. She talked with the person in charge and then made her way towards the three Rosie children. She said, "Would you like to come home with me?" Alex replied for them all, "We'd like it fine."

And very fine it proved to be. Grace Tetlow was a wonderful Christian lady. A widow with one married son. They stayed with her for over a year. She taught them the Lord's Prayer and they went to Sunday School! It was a wonderful time for all the children and was to prove to be an influential part of Bill's life in particular. When they returned home they stopped going to Sunday School; but seeds had been sown that would later bear fruit.

As the time for sitting his Highers drew near Bill started wondering what career he would pursue. The final year group were told of a government scheme to train and fast-track engineers, who were much needed as the country recovered from the effects of the war. Bill with another lad decided to apply. It meant spending three days taking exams at Edinburgh University. Bill was successful in the exams and was called for interview and various tests in Glasgow.

When the final results came through Bill was given a place in the Ministry of Supply factory in Leeds. And so it was that Bill left Edinburgh and moved to Leeds. The factory had arranged for him to stay in a boarding house.

There came a time when with three other apprentices Bill looked for a youth club. They found the youth club of the nearby Halton Methodist Church. They were well received by the young people, and the minister invited the group to Church. Bill and another lad gladly accepted and started to attend. Halton Methodist Church, on the outskirts of Leeds, was where I met Bill not long after he started attending.

Strangely, our paths had come close to crossing in Edinburgh. The school Bill attended as a boy was opposite where my Dad kept his Brooke Bond van. The lads, including Bill, often played on the vans and the drivers often had to send them away. It is quite possible that Dad sent Bill packing! Grandma's house was close to the primary school that Bill attended. Bill, with other lads, often walked on the high wall at the bottom of her back garden! My cousin Charlie attended the same primary school but was in an older group. But they had a common friend called Geoffrey Squires! My Dad sold tea to a shop owned by friends of Bill's parents and Ma Rosie often visited her friends!

God had said something else to me in Reading that was also to have an important bearing on my future. Dad had asked me to leave teaching and help him start a shop. I had said, "No. Teaching is my vocation." But at Reading God said, "Think of all your Dad has done for you. Can you not do this for him?" When I returned to Leeds I said, "I'll help you , Dad."

"That's what I've been waiting for," he answered, and started looking for a business to buy. He found it in the mining village of Aylesham in East Kent. It could hardly have been further away from Leeds! Mum and Dad went down to Aylesham to start the business. Dickie was being looked after by Aunt Louie in Edinburgh. David was away teaching. I had to continue teaching to work my notice for

three months, so I went into digs and every moment I could see Bill I did. I promised Dad I would help him for two and a half years and then would get married. Bill agreed it would be the right thing to do.

At Easter Bill and I had a short holiday in Keswick and then went up to Edinburgh so that I could collect Dickie to take him down to Aylesham. While in Edinburgh we went to a Seventh Day Adventist meeting with Aunt Louie to hear a well-known speaker. He preached on "Believe and be baptised". It was the first sermon I had heard on believers' baptism. I was immediately convinced. When I got to Aylesham I found that the Baptist Church was to hold a baptismal service in two weeks' time! There was no Methodist Church in the village and my parents were attending the Baptist Church. I went to see the minister and told him of my conviction about being baptised. He agreed to baptise me.

I tried to get used to my new life in the draper's shop but I missed Bill very much. If only I could see him once more before I settled down to being without him for what seemed like eternity. There could only be a few brief holidays during the next two and a half years. Dad understood my feelings and allowed me to take a weekend off to see Bill. Together we faced up to what we knew was God's will for the next two and a half years. We promised to write every second day and we parted once more for our separate lives. Little did I know that Aylesham was to prove a training ground unimagined in its opportunities and scope.

5

"God, fill me with Your Spirit"

Coal was discovered in East Kent in the 1920s and in the 1930s miners came from the traditional mining areas of Scotland, Wales, the North East and Yorkshire. During the depression many were out of work. Some had been sacked, some were on the run, many were unemployed through no fault of their own. From such a source came the work force for the mines of East Kent. Houses were built for the miners and Aylesham soon became like a pioneer town in the 'Wild West'. There was a lot of violence, immorality, heavy drinking and gambling. The bank that was opened was used by so few that it soon closed. By the time we reached the village there was a population of seven thousand.

Aylesham developed its own accent. With a conglomeration of Welsh, Scots and Geordie among the adults, the children developed a unique dialect. My brother David married an Aylesham girl and they went as missionaries to Nigeria. While they were there they went to a gathering where there were folk from the UK. One of them turned to Meg, David's wife, and said, "I know where you come from. You come from Aylesham in East Kent"! He had spent some time in the RAF in East Kent and had met some of the Aylesham girls.

By the time we arrived the place had settled down somewhat but the people had their tales to tell of the early years of the mine.

"They kept coal in the bath and chopped the door down for firewood!"

"I was coming home one night and I saw an axe being thrown

31

between two houses. They were always at loggerheads."

Some of the folk were rough but you knew where you stood with them. It was refreshingly different from the pious and sometimes hypocritical respectability of the people in Edinburgh. I had reacted against this as a child without knowing why. We loved the Aylesham people and got to know them well as they shared their lives with us in the draper's shop.

Shortly after my baptism the Baptist Minister left to minister in another church. The Manse, which was one of the few non-pit houses in the village, became empty. The church was not anticipating getting another minister in the near future, so we were offered it to rent. This was an answer to prayer. We had been living in a little two-bedroom flat and the larger accommodation of the Manse was ideal for our needs.

Mum was asked to play the organ and Dad to teach in the Sunday School. I started a weekly Prayer Meeting, preached regularly and started a Young People's Fellowship. At the beginning there were just seven girls, but we felt it should be a mixed group. At an East Kent Young Baptist Association (EKYBA) conference we attended, each group was asked: "What do you want prayer for?"

I spoke up, "Boys!"

Everybody laughed; but it seems they prayed and soon boys began to attend the group. At the time I started the group there was only one other Christian – Jessie. When I shared my testimony with her she said, "So *that's* what happened to me!" She had had the experience of conversion but hadn't known how to vocalise it.

One by one the others came to the Lord. Three came as a result of an experience I had in Canterbury Cathedral. I had been reading books about the fullness of the Holy Spirit and I wanted the experience for myself. I was in Canterbury one day and wandered into the cathedral. I knelt in the little Thomas à Becket Chapel and prayed, "God, fill me with Your Spirit." There were no flashes of lightning, no voices from Heaven. As an act of faith I rose from my knees believing that what I had asked for had been given.

Next morning I had a letter from Bill. He told me he had been filled with God's Spirit! We had been hundreds of miles apart yet we had experienced the same blessing at more or less the same time! Bill's letter went on, "Now that I am completely His I must obey Him in all things. I want to see you at Christmas but I don't know yet if it is in God's plan." We had spent a week together in the summer. It was now November and we were both looking forward to some days together at Christmas. I looked at the situation with new eyes. So this is what is meant by being filled with the Spirit! I had gone into it without counting the cost. I knelt down in my bedroom. "Whatever it costs, Lord, I want to be filled with Your Spirit."

I was speaking at a young people's meeting in Canterbury the next day. I gave an evangelistic message and made an appeal. They came forward and queued up to be led to Jesus. I lost count that night of the number I introduced to the Saviour! As I journeyed home in the train I thought, 'What a wonderful meeting. The leaders must have been praying a lot.' It never occurred to me that I had anything to do with what had happened!

The next evening my friend Heather from the Young People's Fellowship came to see me about books she was reading before going to College. I had been longing to see Heather come through for the Lord. That night she did! It took four hours!

Heather said, "If I become a Christian would I have to go abroad and be a missionary?"

"If He asked you to," I said.

"I want to be a teacher," she stressed.

I assured her that Jesus knew best, and as the desire to be a Christian grew in her the Holy Spirit came upon her. She began to cry, as a sense of sin overwhelmed her. She surrendered her life to Jesus and was changed in a moment. We became good friends and God did eventually call her to go to Africa as a missionary where she worked for many years.

A couple of nights later my friend Phyllis, one of the 'seven', came to see me. The same thing happened! Then Margaret, another of the

'seven', also committed her life to Christ. Only then did I realise that with the fullness of the Holy Spirit I had found a new power in witnessing. These three friends were the firstfruits of my deeper commitment. Eventually all the 'seven' became Christians and so did some of the young men who had joined the group. Some came from really rough backgrounds, but they were chosen by God and became strong Christians. In time some of them were to spread to different parts of the world to serve Jesus. We joined with other young Baptists in East Kent and were always regarded as fun-loving but deeply spiritual Christians who were keen to win others and unafraid to witness for Jesus.

In the shop we found many opportunities to help others. They came to us with their problems, some of which we had never encountered before.

"I can't stand it any more," said one woman as she sat on the chair by the counter.

"Can't stand what?" I asked.

"It's my husband. He brings his mates home and they pay him to have sex with me! I tell you I just can't stand it any more!"

It was at Aylesham that I started my first Girls' Club. We had various interests like crafts and sports, but always there was a devotional emphasis. Jessie helped me and one summer we decided to take the girls camping. Neither of us had been camping before. We only had one tent between us but we managed to borrow all manner of tents, little covers and one that was no more than a soldier's cape! We got permission from a farmer to camp in one of his fields. We gathered wood for an open fire and used an abandoned foxhole for a toilet! God was kind to us. The weather was good and we planned a full programme, and all went according to plan. We learned a lot and the girls grew in their love for Jesus. It was a thoroughly enjoyable experience.

One of the girls in the club was Margaret. She had an independent and lively nature and could lead others astray. She didn't know Jesus and I often despaired of her. Finally I banned her from the club. She reminded me of this years later, when as a fine Christian girl, now totally committed to Christ, she married my brother! It was not my habit to ban children from any organisation. In my Sunday School class I had a lovable rogue who would often play me up. Other teachers suggested I "throw him out", but I never did. I felt he had great potential. I was saddened to find after returning from holiday that the Sunday School Superintendent had expelled him.

Whilst at Aylesham I learned a valuable lesson on platonic friendships. In the church was a man, a divorcee and twenty years older than me. He often seemed on the brink of a deepening commitment to Jesus. I felt I could help Harry. He invited me to his home where he lived with his mother, and he gave me painting lessons. A friendship developed and we sometimes went out together. On my part it was a purely platonic friendship, but I found out that he had fallen in love with me. He was a 'gentleman' and never suggested anything more than friendship, knowing I was engaged to Bill. I felt sorry for him and wished I could split myself and marry him as well! I learned a valuable lesson. Platonic friendships hardly ever work and counselling should be done on the basis male with male and female with female. Bill and I have practised this ever since.

We formed a ministry group from the Young People's Fellowship and took youth meetings and services. Before music groups became popular in churches we pioneered this form of worship. We had guitars, a violin and other instruments to lead the singing. We gave testimonies and preached, and then were used to encourage some of the smaller churches in East Kent. One night the young man who was leading in prayer suddenly fainted when he had hardly started to pray. Bill was on holiday and was part of the group leading the service. He stepped forward and finished the prayer while two other lads carried the unconscious lad into the vestry. No one in the

congregation noticed! It was an indication of the deep sense of oneness that the group had to be able to act as they did, without a word needing to be spoken.

The beautiful Kent countryside was idyllic – the hop-fields, the fruit trees, the lazy continental warmth of hot summer days with the low-flying bats and the troublesome July bugs that would fly on to your hair. When Bill came for holidays, which were neither frequent nor long, we would walk along the road to the Spinney, wandering among the trees, sitting, talking, and praying. I made a little chapel there with a cross of branches and would go and pray there when Bill had gone back to Leeds. We kept our promise and wrote every second day, telling each other all we'd been doing and thinking.

Two and a half years seemed a long time to be engaged, living hundreds of miles apart, having little opportunity to spend time together, but it did pass. At last our wedding day came! All the church was invited to the wedding: the young people and the Girls' Club as well as relatives and friends from a distance. There were a hundred guests at the reception. Rationing was still in force and it must have been very difficult for Mum to plan the reception. She did it all herself and provided a lovely meal – though how she did it I shall never know.

We were both aware of the significance of the day and disliked the popular idea of it being "the Bride's day". I wanted it to be as much Bill's day as mine and told him I'd wear a white dress if he wore a black suit. And so it was. We deliberately broke the traditional wedding superstitions, for as Christians we strongly denied they had any significance. My brother David was best man, my friend Doreen was my first bridesmaid and Joan representing the young people was the other.

The speeches at the wedding reception were like a testimony meeting. The speakers were Dad, Bill, David and Aunt Louie, and in different ways they brought God right into the centre of the celebrations. We were so very, very happy.

After the reception we went to London by train and stayed our first night at the Grosvenor Hotel. It was such a special night, we wanted it to be a special place, but it was somewhat formal and cold. We much preferred the guest house in Tiverton in Devon where we spent the rest of the week. After the week we made our way to Leeds and to our first home.

There was still a great housing shortage, even though the war had been over seven years. People had kept asking us where we were going to live, and we would say, "We don't know, but we're trusting God to provide." And He did. Three months before we were due to marry, Bill received a letter from someone he had never met but who had been talking to a friend of ours. The sender said she had heard that Bill was getting married soon and was looking for a place to live. She had a flat that had now become vacant. Would we like it? When Bill saw it he recognised this was God's provision and said he would move in right away. It was near to the factory where Bill worked. It was an attic bed-sitting room with the landing made into a kitchen. It was small, but it was to prove a happy place to start our married life together.

6

Married at last!

When we were married, the Minister, Vivian Evans from Canterbury, gave us the text: "Seek ye first the kingdom of God and His righteousness and all these things shall be added unto you" (Matt. 6:33 KJV). Before we had been married a fortnight we had proved this to be true, so I wrote out the verse and hung it on the wall. Bill got less than £5 per week as an engineering apprentice and we had to pay £2 for the flat. However, this included gas, electricity and coal which was still rationed. The year was 1952. Mum and Dad had given us £50 for a wedding present, but that was for furniture which we didn't need immediately because the flat was furnished, so we felt we couldn't touch that. However, as a symbol that we felt our home should be an open home, we bought two chairs so that we could invite guests. Another item of furniture we bought was a bookcase in the sales. Otherwise we bought nothing more and learned to live on our income.

On Saturday nights we went to a young people's meeting where we met for fellowship and then went into the town and held an open-air meeting. Anyone interested we took back to our meeting place. It was good training in evangelism. Afterwards we returned home and on the way bought fish and chips for supper. If we couldn't afford fish we would get a fish-cake. If that proved too dear then chips alone would suffice; but if that proved impossible, we went home to a plate of cornflakes! We allowed ourselves to buy a quarter pound of

toffees each week and from the bag we had one toffee each. The rest were put in a tin so that we had something to give our landlady's children at Christmas. We were poor financially but rich in love for each other and the knowledge of God's love. We attended a class to learn New Testament Greek; we read to each other in bed at night; went for walks and, occasionally, went to the cinema. Every Sunday we went to church and invited friends home.

Our landlady, Nellie, had a Jehovah's Witness come to see her every Monday evening. Nellie didn't always understand what was said to her, so she asked me to attend with her. This I did and started challenging the visitor about some of her statements. She then asked another lady higher in the organisation to join us. She told me in no uncertain terms, "You're heading for Armageddon!" Nellie soon saw the errors and asked the lady to stop coming. I was overjoyed when she committed her life to Christ.

In the spring of 1953 Bill's younger sister Jessie came to stay for a holiday. She wasn't a Christian and I longed to share Jesus with her, but I hesitated. Was this the right time? Was she ready? One morning I put this questioning to the Lord. In my Bible reading were the words, "Woman, great is thy faith, be it unto thee even as thou wilt." I knew my prayer had been answered. Bill was already at work. As Jessie was having breakfast I told her about Jesus. She responded and asked Jesus to be her Saviour. Later she married Don, an American serviceman, and went to live in the United States. We have visited her on a number of occasions. She has never forgotten that day she surrendered her life to Jesus in our little flat. We had the joy of witnessing to Don when some years later he died of cancer. He died trusting in Jesus.

I fully expected that soon after we got married I would become pregnant, and was disappointed that this was not so. However, after three months I began to feel sick in the mornings. I didn't realise this was the first sign! When I told Nellie how I was feeling she told me that it looked as though I was pregnant. It was soon confirmed and I looked forward eagerly to our firstborn. We bought a second-hand

pram and I started to knit some woollies and, as we could afford, began to buy other clothes. I began to feel a little homesick. No doubt it was due to the pregnancy, because I was very happy. I wanted to see Mum and Dad again, so we planned to go down to Aylesham for Christmas. We tried to save the fare but in the end we had to take the money out of the bank.

It was lovely seeing Mum and Dad again, but it was almost as if they had forgotten I had lived with them. They would say things like, "We always have porridge at breakfast", and I felt like saying, "I know. I used to live here." It made me realise I no longer belonged with them. My life was with Bill. I never felt homesick again.

I enjoyed the pregnancy. The early morning sickness soon passed and I felt well. I put on much more weight than I had expected and became so big that the doctor began to wonder if I was having twins. X-rays were taken – two babies! It was fascinating to see the X-ray – like two little sardines in a tin: one with the head down and the other with the head up! I normally weighed eight and a half stones. I went up to nearly twelve before the twins were born. At seven months I was taken into hospital for two weeks. Nothing was wrong but it was felt I should have a rest and also to see me over that critical time when twins can be born early. I quite enjoyed it and it was indeed restful.

The day before the twins were due – July 3rd – I attended the antenatal clinic and they found my blood pressure was high due to toxaemia. I was told this could be dangerous for the babies. "Come in tomorrow and we'll start you off." This I duly did and was induced. Mary, the 'head-down' baby, wasn't ready to be born and although the midwife shouted and slapped me and told me to push, nothing happened. Finally I was taken into the operating theatre and given a general anaesthetic. Surrounded by nurses and doctors I fell asleep. Mary had to be turned and delivered by forceps. Ruth followed quickly even though she was born breach. Mary had made the way for her. Mary weighed 5lb 11oz but Ruth was only 3lb 14oz and was so dopey with the anaesthetics from the induction and the

actual birth, that it took them three quarters of an hour to get her breathing properly.

When I woke up I was on my own. I felt my tummy. It was flat, so the twins must have been delivered. But where were they? Were they boys or girls or one of each? Soon I was told they were girls and I was taken to the ward. But it was to be two days before I saw them. My blood pressure was very high and it was not safe to move me. I was told the twins were in incubators.

I was glad it was all over, but sad that I had been unable to give birth in a natural way. I felt that somehow I had let God down. It was explained to me that it was in no way any fault of mine. The midwife apologised to me for the way she had treated me.

"I'm sorry about slapping you," she said. "You couldn't give birth naturally because the first baby needed to be turned."

Bill, of course, was able to see the babies the evening after their birth and he described them to me. After two days, Mary was taken from the incubator and was brought to me. What a beautiful baby! She was just as Bill had described. Olive-coloured skin, big blue eyes and golden hair. Ruth was still in an incubator and they took me to see her a few days later. She looked just like Mary only much smaller. She looked very frail until I looked at the other incubators and saw the other babies, who were premature and undeveloped. Ruth was small but full term and healthy. She stayed in the incubator for two weeks, putting weight on well. It was wonderful having both babies with me in the ward. When Ruth was 5lb in weight the doctors said we could go home. We stayed in hospital for nearly three weeks, but my blood pressure continued to be high. We were only allowed home because Aunt Louie was coming to look after us.

My blood pressure remained very high for some time. I was confined to bed. At first I fed both twins together, but then Ruth needed more frequent feeds. She was fed three hourly and Mary four hourly during the night as well as the day. This posed a big problem for Bill, because I was on pills for my blood pressure to make me

sleep. The alarm clock was set for various times during the night and Bill had to prop me up on pillows and hand me the twin that was to be fed.

Bill began to have nightmares! "Glad," he'd call. "I've lost Ruth!" He'd be searching for her under the bed when all the time she was safely in her cot! We laugh about it now.

Gradually my blood pressure went down and I was allowed to get up. Louie returned to Scotland. Mum came on the 9th of August for a week and was a great help. Bill's Mum also came and spent some time with us. The twins were dedicated in the little Methodist Church we attended. At the end of the service, as if in blessing, Ruth lifted her hand! We prayed that that would be a sign of things to come, that the Lord would use them to bless others.

Life was a bit crowded and difficult for us in the flat. No modern aids for washing the nappies, sheets, towels, etc. I had to carry the washing down two flights of stairs to the garden. The same thing happened when I put the twins out to sleep in the fresh air. With only one room we were rather crushed. Aunt Louie, Mum and Bill's Mum had to sleep in a put-u-up in the kitchen! How glad we were when our dear friend Annie, who had been Bill's landlady, invited us to stay in their house for a fortnight while they were on holiday. We packed as much as we could in the twin pram (which Bill had bought to replace the single pram) and I pushed that while Bill carried the big case and the baby bath. We felt like pioneers setting out for the Wild West with our canopy-covered pram looking like a covered wagon! The Lord had provided yet again. We were so happy and grateful for all His provision.

When I began to get up and move around again, I lost some of my milk and only had enough for one baby, so it was suggested they be treated alike and fed alternately breast and bottle. It was a wonderful solution! It meant that when Bill was at home he could feed the one on the bottle. We also bathed them at night so they got used to the love and attention of both parents. How happy we were! So much in love with each other, with the Lord and our dear little girls. It was all so complete.

7

Back to Kent

National Service had been postponed for Bill while he did his apprenticeship, but it finally came. When the twins were five months old he was called up to serve his Queen and country for two years. Mum and Dad invited me and the twins to stay with them, so we made the long journey to Kent at the beginning of December 1953. Bill and I made a twin carry-cot to take the twins on the train. They loved the rocking of the train. Dad met us in London and we crossed the capital by taxi. Another train journey to Canterbury and Dad's car took us to Aylesham.

We had one day together before Bill left, and I felt very depressed. Somehow all the problems and difficulties ahead of me mounted before my eyes and I wept when we were alone. Bill worked hard to get as much as possible done for me and by the afternoon I felt much better. At 4.30 on Thursday morning Bill left for the R.E.M.E. camp at Honiton in Devon. I went back to bed feeling – nothing. Somehow that day my heart would not feel, but there was much to do and I kept myself busy. By Saturday the tears were very near and I tried not to think of my beloved; but I felt strengthened as I started the day with the Lord and He said, "Be strong and of a good courage". It was encouraging, too, to remember that God never allows us to be tested beyond what we can bear (1 Cor 10:13). This has always been a life principle with me and proved to be a great source of comfort.

Unexpectedly, Bill came home for a fortnight's leave over

Christmas. The Commanding Officer of the camp felt it was wrong to call up men so near to Christmas, so he sent everybody home for two weeks of unscheduled leave! It was a wonderful bonus for Christmas. My brother David also came home. What a happy company we were! Mum and Dad gave the twins high chairs and they enjoyed being higher in the world and having things to play with on their trays. We had photographs taken of the four of us before we left Leeds and it was lovely to have an enlarged one of Bill to show the twins when he went back.

It was some time before Bill was able to get home, and the twins forgot who he was. They cried at the stranger who picked them up and his tears flowed too. I missed him so much, but the presence of the twins who were so much a part of him comforted me and brought great joy. We had been apart for two and a half years during our engagement and this further separation was hard to bear.

As the days got warmer I took the twins for a walk nearly every day up Spinney Lane, our favourite walk where Bill and I had spent many happy hours courting. It was all so beautiful with a wood on one side and clearings of grass – lovely little spots where one can picnic or sunbathe or read a book.

Being back in Aylesham meant that I was able to pick up the leadership of the young people again on a Friday evening. Mum and Dad baby-sat and it was good to have a break from the twins. Bill was able to have a fortnight's leave that summer on compassionate grounds to help with the twins, and it was such a joy to be together again. There were times, too, when he hitch-hiked from Honiton to get at least part of a weekend with us.

After the first year Bill passed his long training in field wireless and was due to be posted. He had been told that he would be attached to No. 1 Anti-Aircraft Artillery based at Woolwich. This was so much nearer Aylesham and we were both thrilled at the prospect. When he went to collect his travel warrant, however, he found that he had been misinformed. He was not going to No. 1 Anti-Aircraft Artillery at Woolwich, but No. 1 Coast Artillery at Dover – just a few

miles from Aylesham!

There was no time to contact me before his train left. He duly reported to the Camp Commander at Dover. He noted that Bill's home address was Aylesham and said, "Go home to Aylesham and I'll see you in the morning"!

It was a wonderful surprise when Bill appeared at the door! How good of the Lord to provide for us in this way. More was to be revealed of God's provision. We learned that we could hire a house and the army would pay for the accommodation up to a rent of £3 a week. We found a furnished house to rent in Shepherd's Well, a delightful village between Aylesham and Dover and the rent was £3 a week!

How glad we were to be together again. Bill got home each evening about 5.30 pm and weekends were free except for the occasional duty. It was just as if he were in a civilian job. The twins had a bedroom of their own and there was a lovely big garden where they could play. That summer was hot, with cloudless skies for six weeks. I was forever taking photographs of the twins in the garden; they were so cute and pretty. During that six weeks Bill was away at Felixstowe where he was looking after radio controlled boats that the coast artillery used for target practice, but there was not the level of pain I had previously experienced. I knew he would be home again soon and that before Christmas he would be demobbed.

We began to think of our future. Bill had received a call from the Lord to the ministry and had begun 'pushing doors'. He went for an interview regarding acceptance in the July. The wheels had begun to turn towards full-time ministry. As demob approached Bill was informed by the camp C.O. that he had heard there was a job vacancy for a draughtsman-surveyor with British Rail based at Ashford in Kent. He shared it with me and we felt that he should see what was involved. He was given leave by the C.O. to attend an interview and Bill was duly offered the job. We felt that here again was a wonderful provision by the Lord.

That Christmas was a very happy time for us all. For the first time the twins were able to enter into some understanding of it. On Christmas Eve the girls hung up two of Daddy's socks, different colours so they could identify them later. When they had gone to bed, we decorated the room and the Christmas tree. Their stockings were filled. Bill had made a farmhouse and farm workers and animals were placed appropriately. He had made beds for the dolls and I had made bedding for them. Other presents were around the tree. In the morning they came down and stood open-mouthed at the transformation of the room.

We had told them that it was Jesus' birthday and they picked up some sticks with streamers and went round the room chanting, "Hooray! It's Jesus's birthday!"

We terminated the rental agreement with the house in Shepherd's Well and moved to a house in Canterbury. This was conveniently placed for easy access to Ashford and also to Aylesham. The house was close to the centre of Canterbury and was over three hundred years old! There was no front garden but there was a lovely long garden going down to the river. Opposite was an island with an apple orchard. It was as if we were in the middle of the country! It was delightful! There was a lounge, dining room, kitchen and toilet downstairs and three bedrooms upstairs. As with all the old houses in Canterbury the upstairs floors were uneven, but it just added character to the place. The house only cost £400 because there were plans to redevelop the site some years in the future. We hadn't that amount of money but Dad and David lent it to us and we paid them rent.

For the first time we had to buy furniture, so we scoured the second-hand shops. Again the Lord provided. At the Auction Sale Rooms we got a beige Saxony carpet for £7 and a matching three-piece suite for £3, so we furnished the lounge for £10! The following May we went camping and my two brothers David and Dickie came too. How Mary and Ruth enjoyed it – sleeping in a tent, eating

dinner on the grass, picking flowers in the wood and finding a bird's nest were all causes for great excitement. They settled down to camping as if born to it.

In July Elisabeth was born; a dark haired, dark blue-eyed baby girl weighing 7lb 4oz. I gave birth to her at home and it was an easy birth. She had quite a lot of hair and with her big bright eyes she reminded us of Enid Blyton's Noddy! She was a very placid baby and learned to sleep through the night at two days old!

I was grateful to have various people come and give help to get me on my feet again. Margaret, David's future wife, came for ten days and Bill was on holiday for the second week. Then my friend Heather came for a few days. In August Bill had to go away for two weeks army training as a 'refresher course' for his National Service. It proved to be at a very critical time, because the Suez Crisis occurred just in that period and some reservists were quickly called up. We praised God that Bill came home after the two weeks and we proved again that "all things work together for good to them that love God" (Romans 8: 28 KJV).

In the spring of that eventful year Dad began to feel pain in his stomach. At first he thought it was indigestion, but it persisted so he went to the doctor, who sent him to the hospital. Tests proved he had cancer. He was operated on, but it was found that the cancer had spread to the liver. I remember phoning the hospital to ask how he was.

"We found he was inoperable so we just sewed him up again" was the stark reply.

It was the same week that Elisabeth was born. Sadness and joy mingled together. We prayed a lot for Dad's recovery and he believed himself to be healed. He even got up from bed one day and scrubbed the kitchen floor to show that belief. The doctor had told us that we were not to tell him that the operation had not been successful. We found this difficult, as we had not, as a family, been in the habit of lying to each other. Finally, Mum told him.

47

David took Dad to the West Country to see Peter Scothern, who had a ministry of healing. He didn't pray for Dad's healing but cast an evil spirit out of him. That night Dad passed something out of himself in the toilet, which he believed was the cancer. However, he continued to deteriorate and became just skin and bone. He became too weak even to lift a grape to his lips.

Dad had never thought much about Heaven, as he had always said he followed Jesus because he loved Him and not for what he could get out of it. Our minister came to see him every week and one day Dad said to him, "Mr Evans, when I die will I sit on a cloud all day and play a harp?"

"Certainly not," came the reply. "You'll be serving God in Heaven."

"I'm so glad," Dad replied, "I like to be busy."

When he came to die it was with a word of thanks to Mum and a joke. She brought him a drink and he thanked her, and then said, "That's the way to do it!" quoting Punch.

At first when I knew he had died I couldn't believe it and decided that God was going to do a greater miracle. Dave and I went into the room where he lay in his coffin and, laying aside the grave clothes, we took his hand and said, "In the name of Jesus, Dad get up." It was only when they nailed down the coffin lid that I accepted it.

A letter came from Heather. She, too, had difficulty accepting his death. He had been doing so much good work, particularly among the young people. "Why?" she asked in prayer. Then the Lord showed her a vision of Jesus coming up to him in Heaven, putting His arm around his shoulder and saying, "It's good to see you, Dick." When I read the letter I finally accepted that Jesus wanted him – and who was I to want to keep him here?

Three-year-old Mary and Ruth loved their little baby sister and were so happy doing little things to help me. One day Jack, from the Aylesham young people's fellowship which we still led, came to see us. Elisabeth was in her pram. As he was leaving he said, "Oh well,

I'll just take this baby with me," and he wheeled the pram towards the front door.

"No you can't!" said Ruth, bursting into tears. "She's *our* baby!"

We had a cat called Kitty and the girls loved her. She had several litters (usually in the toy cupboard!) and the kittens were also a source of delight. The garden was lovely and I often put a large rug on the grass under the old apple tree so that Elisabeth could sit there and the twins would play with their toys. While we were in Canterbury we went on three holidays, one camping with David and Dickie, one to Broadstairs where we enjoyed the beach and another to Leamington Spa.

One day whilst we were still living in Canterbury I was reading an article about the plight of prostitutes, and my eyes filled with tears. I wept for those girls. The Lord gave me a burden for them and I knew I had to do something to help them. I shared this with Bill and we agreed that it would be right to share it with the young people's group at Aylesham, which we now ran jointly.

They were a strong group of dedicated young men and women and together we developed a strategy for action. They came to our house one Saturday evening. We spent an hour in prayer and then went out in twos with tracts to witness in the streets. Two stayed to babysit and as I left the house I shouted back, "Put the kettle on. We'll bring them back for a cuppa." It was to prove the beginning of a momentous adventure for Jesus that was to last for the next eighteen months.

That first Saturday evening I went out into the streets of Canterbury with Margaret, my future sister-in-law. We spoke to a couple of lads standing at a street corner. We offered them a tract and spoke to them about Jesus. They told us their names were Don and Scratch! They were interested in talking about Jesus and we invited them back to the house.

Don told us his story. He lived in a village outside Canterbury and had woken up that morning with the feeling that something special

was going to happen that day. He went into Canterbury and entered a coffee bar – nothing special there. He went into the cinema, watched a film for a bit and got bored, so he left. Then he met Scratch whom he had never met before. They started talking and it was at this point we met them. Don was ready to open his heart to the Lord and, after an hour or two sharing and teaching, Bill had the joy of leading him to the Lord. He told us he had had a girlfriend called Joyce whom he had ridiculed because she went to church.

"I wish I could meet her now," he said, "and tell her how sorry I am."

Then he asked if he could join us next week and go out into the streets to talk to people. It was arranged that he would go out with my brother David.

There were others who came that night and soon every Saturday our house was full of young people in all the downstairs rooms and on the stairs. On the whole they were Teddy Boys who came. There were some soldiers, sailors and one prostitute, "Canterbury Lil". We never saw Scratch again. His real name was Filmer, which didn't match the image he wanted for himself, so he became Scratch.

Don did come back the following week and went out on to the streets with David. They met Joyce! She came back to the house and also committed her life to Jesus. In time Don and Joyce got married and became members of the Methodist Church Joyce had previously attended. They developed a ministry showing Christian films to various groups.

A few weeks after we started we had two unexpected callers one Sunday. They introduced themselves as detectives who were investigating a robbery at a local fish and chip shop near us the previous evening. We invited them in.

One of the men explained: "We questioned some lads who are known to us and who were in the area. They said it wasn't them. They then said that they were in your house at the time and you were talking to them about Jesus! Knowing these lads as we do we felt this was a pack of lies; but they insisted it was so."

"Who were they?" we asked.

They told us their names and we said, "Yes. It's true. They were here until gone midnight and we *were* talking to them about Jesus."

The detectives were amazed! Later some young soldiers from the local barracks were arrested for the robbery. An important result from this incident was that the police now knew that gangs of Teddy Boys walking up Stour Street on a Saturday were *not* a cause for concern!

Canterbury is thought of as a religious city with the magnificent cathedral dominating the skyline. We discovered, however, that violence and crime were very real problems. One Saturday as Bill was on his way towards the main street he met two lads who had obviously been in a fight. He recognised them as lads who had been to our house. One lad had blood all over his shirt.

"Are you all right?" Bill asked.

"Oh, yes," he answered. "It's the other fellow's blood not mine!"

The possibility of violence erupting in our house was always there, but we got utter respect from the lads and any tiffs that developed were soon stopped.

It was mostly teenagers and young men who came. A number of them dressed in their Teddy Boy gear. There were a few girls and we found them even tougher than the lads. Because the Aylesham young people knew each other so well they were able to throw the conversation round the room to each other and guide the discussion to the best advantage. We always had an hour of prayer together before going out, to ensure that God was central in all we were seeking to do. It was recognised that this time of prayer was the key to any success in sharing Jesus with those we met. It was also a great bonding time for us all.

One of the things we stressed was that violence was not the way to solve relationship problems. "It takes more guts NOT to fight" was one of the things we stressed. One Saturday as we were praying there was a knock at the door. There was a bigger gathering of lads wanting to come in than we had ever had. Some we knew but others

were strangers. We told them they were too early. We made it very clear. "We're praying. Come back in an hour."

They had learned to trust us and knew we were not fobbing them off. "OK," they said and went off, but came back and filled the house! It seems that earlier that afternoon the Canterbury Teddy Boys met up with the Faversham Teddy Boys. The two sides were taunting each other and it looked as though they would get into a fight. Before they got to that point one of the Canterbury lads said to the Faversham gang, "We go to a house on Saturday nights and we talk about Jesus."

You can imagine the derision from the Faversham lads! The lad persisted.

"One of the things they say is that it takes more guts **not** to fight than it does to fight," he said. "Why not come along and meet our friends."

And they came! Every conceivable space was used. There was no agro but there was plenty of talk about Jesus and the change He can make in our lives.

We made it a policy never to ask them to leave. This was a hard decision, but knowing that these lads were forever being told to move on, we determined to show that they were accepted by us and accepted by Jesus. It was usually the early hours of Sunday morning when the last would leave and sometimes they even stayed the night! One lad, who was in the navy, would come to us first when he had a few days leave. He would stay the night and make us breakfast, and then go on to meet up with his parents.

If anyone stayed it meant that the twins had to share a bed in order to put someone up. One day I said to Bill, "I'm going to the auction rooms today to see if they have a bed." Bill agreed this was a good idea.

I looked around before the sale began and saw a bed settee. "Great idea," I thought. "That will give extra seating as well as a bed for two." The mattress was good and clean and I felt the Lord say to

me, "You'll get it for thirty shillings (£1.50)." The time for bidding came.

"Ten shillings," I cried out.

"One pound," came from someone.

"Thirty shillings," was my bid, confident that it would be the final bid.

"Two pounds," was called out.

I was taken aback. I was sure the Lord had said I would get it for thirty shillings, and I would not go any higher. The hammer came down, "Sold for two pounds."

When Bill came home that evening and asked about the settee I said, "I don't understand it. I was sure the Lord said I would get it for thirty shillings, but it went for two pounds."

Next morning a letter arrived from the auctioneer telling us that the person who bid two pounds was the owner of the settee trying to push up the price. As I was the last to bid I could have it for thirty shillings! It became a very useful part of our furniture.

Before Bill left the army he had begun the process of seeking acceptance for training for the Baptist Ministry. He was accepted for training and given a place at the Baptist College that was then at Rawden near Leeds. There were no facilities for families, so the prospect was that there would be three years of separation. One evening, while Bill was at the young people's meeting I sat on the rug in front of the fire and battled with the Lord. "Must there be another separation, Lord?" I asked. But the heavens seemed empty. Like Abraham of old with his only son, God waited for my willingness. I wept. I struggled. Before the evening was through I told the Lord I was willing. However, as with Abraham, it was not needed.

Bill had applied for an education grant while we were still at Shepherd's Well and it was more or less agreed that he would get the grant from the Kent County Education Authority. When we moved to Canterbury we discovered that we had left the jurisdiction of Kent County Education Authority and were now under the Canterbury

Education Authority. No grant would be available from the County! Bill would have to start the long, involved process all over again! However, in a wonderful way the Baptist Union accepted that Bill could qualify for ministry using an alternative scheme of exams where the tuition is by correspondence course. That meant that Bill could do this study while having a pastorate. This alternative was more acceptable to us, but it would be far more difficult for Bill.

He started his study while he was still an engineer with British Rail. There came a time when the District Engineer asked to see Bill in his office. When Bill went to see him the District Engineer said that there was a post coming up that would suit him very well. There was a big increase in salary and a very real step up the ladder. One of the perks would be first class rail travel for the family throughout Europe! He said the post had to be advertised through the rail regions but, since he appointed the person, he wanted Bill to have it!

Bill thanked him and said he would think about it. He shared it with me and we wondered what it all meant. It was at this time that Bill had been to visit the Whetstone Baptist Church in South Leicestershire who were looking to appoint a new minister. Shortly before Bill had to give his answer to the District Engineer a letter came from Whetstone inviting him to become their minister. As we read the letter we recognised that the British Rail offer was the temptation of the Devil to deflect from the work God was calling us both to do. We smiled at each other. We didn't need to discuss what to do. Bill went to see the District Engineer and thanked him for his offer, and told him that he would not be applying for the post. In fact Bill gave his notice of leaving and told him he was going to be a Baptist Minister. The District Engineer told him he was a fool! To some, of course, it looked that way. Half the salary for twice the hours! But there was the precious sense of peace that we knew what God wanted.

8

"Don't worry ... I shall provide"

It was the end of February 1958 when we moved to Whetstone in South Leicestershire. It was quite a momentous journey. It was raining as we left Canterbury to catch the train to London. As we changed stations in London it was sleeting. The further north we travelled the heavier was the snow – so that when we reached Leicester there was 5 inches of snow. The deacon who met us at the station informed us that word had come through that our furniture van was stuck in a snowdrift near Northampton and would not be arriving until tomorrow. Arrangements were made for the twins to stay with one family and Elisabeth and ourselves with other members of the church. Right away, despite the weather, we felt at home and knew the warmth of their welcome. We quickly sensed that we were certainly among the people God wanted us to minister to. There was real love there and we never throughout our years there heard them ever speak ill of one another.

The Manse was described (not by them) as "the best Baptist manse in the East Midlands". It was a detached house standing higher than the church next door. There was a large garden with a lawn behind and fruit bushes and trees at the back and the side and a vegetable patch. There were rose bushes at the front of the house and a rockery leading down to the front lawn which we often used for playing croquet. Beyond the front lawn was a grass tennis court and a garage.

It was a lovely garden for the children to play in. Bill made a tree house and Ruth and Mary spent many happy hours playing in it and watching the visitors come and go. We often had picnics on the lawn in the summer.

The severe weather that greeted our arrival lasted throughout March. This was a factor in causing the death of a number of elderly people who were ill. Bill had so many funerals in the first few weeks of his ministry that people referred to him as "the funeral king"! The twins saw a number of funeral cars arriving at the church and so became very aware of funerals. On one occasion when they were looking out of the window they saw the coffin being taken out of the hearse and into the church.

"What's that box for?" asked Mary.

"That's where they put the body," I answered.

"Where do they put the head?" asked Ruth.

The following week we were having tea. Bill was late arriving. The conversation went like this:

Mary: "Daddy's late coming home."

Ruth: "Perhaps he's fallen off his bike."

Mary: "Perhaps he's been killed."

Ruth: "Don't be silly. He can't die yet. He's got to bury all the other people first."!

Bill had to study for his exams but I helped him in regular preaching, visiting and the leading of meetings. The people at Whetstone soon began to realise that I was not going to be the usual Minister's wife, only concerned with women's meetings and organising teas. By his own hard work and dedication Bill was able to pass the exams in four years instead of the usual five.

We had a number of meetings held in the Manse. The young people's meeting on a Monday night, a young wives' group on a Friday night and Deacons' Meetings were all held in the Manse. I led a Girls' Club in the church hall where we had more space for activities, and Bill led a Boys' Club. The Midweek Bible Study

Meeting was also held in the church hall. We had the meetings in the Manse to emphasise that we were church family. From the start we said that we wanted people to call us Bill and Glad. Some found such informality difficult, because they had always referred to the minister and his wife as Reverend and Missus. When we told the Youth Group to call us Bill and Glad there was a stony silence. This was unheard of! After a few awkward seconds one of the teenage lads broke the ice: "OK Bill!" Years later he became Church Secretary.

Audrey was one of the Young People's Fellowship. The first night the group met we discussed "What is a Christian?" We came to the conclusion that a Christian is someone in whom Christ lives. Audrey had been baptised and said, "I believe in Jesus, but I think of Him as living up in Heaven, not living in my life."

I felt very drawn to this frank and open young woman. Next day I wrote her a letter.

Thank you for what you shared with the Youth Group last night. Would you like to come round to the Manse to talk further about what you shared?

I walked up to the building in the village where she worked. I knew the upstairs window where the office was where she would be. I prayed, "Lord, if you want me to give this letter to Audrey send her to the window now." I looked up. I waited just a moment and she appeared at the window! I beckoned her. She came down and I gave her the letter.

That evening she came to the Manse and she accepted Jesus into her life, the firstfruits of the ministry at Whetstone. The interesting thing is that I had misunderstood the directions I had been given about her office. The window did not belong to her office. It was the Boss's! She only went into his office first thing in the morning – except that day!

It was our first Christmas at Whetstone and there were still things we had to do that Christmas Eve to get ready for the morning. The girls were in bed and Bill was putting the finishing touches to a doll's

house he had made for the girls. My one regret was that I had been unable to make a Christmas cake. We just didn't have enough money to buy the ingredients, but we would have a good time none the less. There was a knock at the door and a couple from the next village were there. He was organist at the Blaby Baptist church but his parents and brothers and sisters were very much part of our church. We invited them in.

"We won't stay long," he said. "We want to call and see Mum and Dad. My boss came into the office today and gave me this."

He held up a magnificent Christmas cake with a snow scene with skaters on the ice and little Christmas trees. It was obviously professionally made.

"My boss said, 'Give this to your minister as a present from me.' I told him I had already given a gift to my minister, but if he didn't mind would it be all right if I gave it to you. He said he would be delighted. So Happy Christmas to you and the family." We were reminded, as we had been so often, that God's promise to us on our Wedding Day was that He would provide for us. Each Christmas after that we received a similar cake which came with the best wishes of his boss. His boss was an M.P., though not for our constituency.

We hadn't been at Whetstone long when I had a miscarriage. Liz was just three. I offered the experience to God from the beginning and had perfect peace throughout. The girls in the Young People's Group who visited me were amazed at my tranquillity. God was good to me through that experience. The Lord had given us a promise of a son one day through the words, "You will have a son and you shall call him John." (Luke 1:13) I was not surprised when a few months later I was pregnant again. I was happy at the thought but concerned as to how we would be able to clothe this baby. The stipend was poor, so finances were tight. With five mouths to feed we had to be very careful.

One day I knelt in our bedroom and said, "Lord, how are we going to clothe this new baby?" Distinctly I heard the Lord say to me,

"Don't worry about this child. I shall provide for him." I took God at His word and deliberately did not try to buy new clothes. We still had a couple of nighties, and some vests and nappies left over from Elisabeth. The Lord tested my faith right up to his birth.

The new baby was born at home. The local midwife was a friend of ours and she was happy that Bill should be there during the birth.

"Darling," he told me, "we have a lovely boy!"

What wonderful words to hear! We knew, of course, that he would be called John. It was Saturday when John was born. The date was November 5th, bonfire day. It so happened that next day was the Church Anniversary and our minister from our Kent days, Rev. Vivian Evans, was taking the services. Bill told the church about John's birth and there was genuine joy among the people. Some time before John's birth, the Shah of Persia had had a son and he had cut interest rates for the people as a thanksgiving. Bill said to the people, "I'm sorry I can't give you a tax rebate like the Shah of Persia but I do give you permission every year on John's birthday to celebrate with fireworks and bonfires!'"

Thirty years later, at a rally in the Aston Villa Football Stadium where Desmond Tutu was the speaker, we were sitting beside David, a man who had been one of our congregation at Whetstone. He was now a District Youth Leader for the West Midlands Baptist Association and it was good to meet up with him again. At the end of the Rally there was a tremendous display of fireworks. David turned to us and said, "And to think it's even John's birthday!"

This reference to David reminds me of the day when he and his wife Joyce brought their baby daughter for dedication at Whetstone. Bill had an interesting experience as he was dedicating their baby girl. He felt the Lord say to him, "This baby girl will prove to be a strong Christian and will bless many. She will prove to be a special blessing to her parents and will strengthen their faith." He didn't know whether or not to share this with them. He wondered if it was just a fanciful thought. This was before the charismatic renewal made its impact, and at that time 'words of knowledge' and

'prophecies' were only referred to in Pentecostal Churches. However, he did tell them what he felt God had said. They moved away from Whetstone, but we later met up with them again in the Midlands. When their daughter was 21 we were invited to share in the celebrations. David then shared with us that the word given at her dedication proved true. She had become a very strong Christian and helped many to faith. David and his wife had both slipped from the Lord and were not the vibrant Christians they had been in Whetstone. It was their daughter who brought them back to faith and eventually David exercised a strong ministry among young people.

To get back to our baby John and the words said about provision for him. The ladies of the church started visiting me and they brought gifts for John. Many of them worked in the local knitwear factories and consequently they brought lovely knitted garments – over 30 matinee jackets as well as other things!

To begin with John wore the little nighties that had been Elisabeth's. I put him in the one little romper I had been given, but he needed another. I said to Bill, "I really must go out this afternoon and buy another romper for John." That lunchtime another lady came.

"Sorry I haven't been before but I've been away. I've brought a little gift for John."

It was a romper! That promise of God that He would provide for John went right through his childhood. For instance, Bill's sister Jessie now lived in the United States. She had a son, Scott, who was just slightly older than John. She sent us garments he had grown out of and they fitted John very well. He looked really smart with his American rigouts!

After Dad died Mum lost much of her purpose in living. The sparkle in her life had gone and she felt her only purpose was to look after Dickie. She carried on living in Aylesham but she needed a lot of help running the shop. She developed hardening of the arteries to the brain which caused the brain cells to die. She got more and more

forgetful and began treating Dickie as though he was a little child. She would feed him and see to him at the toilet, things he was perfectly capable of dealing with himself. We realised she couldn't manage on her own. It was decided that Dave and Margaret would return from Nigeria, where they worked as missionaries, and they would take care of her.

They looked after her, Dickie and the shop for a while, but in the end the decision was made to sell the business. Dad had been disappointed that neither David nor I wanted to run it.

David applied for training as a probation officer and, because Mum wanted to stay in Aylesham, we paid for a lady to live in and look after her. However, Mum continued to deteriorate and the time came when the lady felt she could no longer cope with her and Dickie. So it was decided that Mum and Dickie should come to live with us in Whetstone.

It was sad to see how rapidly Mum was deteriorating. She, whom David and I used to refer to as a wise owl and who seemed to know everything, now didn't know who I was. One day I asked her, "Do you remember Dad?"

"Dad?" she said, "my Dad?"

"No, my Dad, Mum. Your husband."

"I don't remember his name," she said, "but we were very happy together. I didn't deserve him."

Quickly all her faculties left her. Even automatic things like opening a door were difficult for her. One day she opened her mouth to say something and "Bla bla, bla," was all that came. I had to bath her. She had the body of a young woman but a mind that seemed so empty. What a contrast to Dad, whose body became so emaciated with cancer that he was unable to lift even a grape to his lips but whose mind remained alert to the end.

One Sunday, amazingly she knew it was Sunday. She put on her gloves (a sure sign she was going to church) and made as if to go to worship, a lifelong practice, but she was still wearing her nightdress! That day she sang the hymn "Trust and obey" right through although

61

she hadn't spoken properly for weeks. On the following Tuesday I helped Mum out of bed to take her to the toilet, but she had forgotten how to walk. I had to walk behind her pushing her legs before me like a zombie. On the Thursday the doctor came.

"What do you think?" he asked.

"I think she's dying," I replied.

He agreed and told me to stop feeding her. I was shocked.

"She can no longer swallow," he said, "and if you feed her the food will lodge in her lungs and she'll get pneumonia."

I rang David with the news and he came over from Mansfield where he was living. He took Dickie to his home so that he wouldn't be around when Mum died. He had grieved so much when Dad died and we couldn't explain things to him. We wanted to spare him. David returned the next day and that night Mum died. Remarkably, she never lost her sweet nature. We rejoiced that now she would have all her faculties again. She was now reunited with Dad. They had loved singing together and now they were reunited, joining in the choir of heaven.

It had not been easy having Mum with us. John was just a baby and the three girls were at school. Dickie, as well as Mum, needed a lot of looking after. Bill helped a lot, particularly with Dickie, but she was my Mum and Dickie was my little brother, so I naturally felt responsible for their welfare. Towards the end the doctor, seeing I was bearing a heavy load, had suggested I put Mum into a care home. I said, "I can't, doctor, she's my mother." I'm glad I never did; but it was only after her death that I realised how tired I was.

It was the hard winter of 1963 when Mum died. One night, shortly before she died, Mum knocked her hot water bottle out of the bed. Her bed was warm but the bottle was frozen solid! The situation in Leicestershire was such that burials could not be held because the ground was so hard. Mum had requested that she be buried with Dad in Aylesham, so we took her body down to Kent where, fortunately, the burial was possible. Although I had left home

years before, it suddenly dawned on me that I was now an orphan and I wept for my loss but more particularly for Mum – such a dear, sweet, patient, gifted and intelligent woman. Her married life had been very happy yet there was much pain. I had frequent illnesses, David had many accidents, Harry had died as a baby and Dickie had Down's Syndrome. After Dad died and she was left with Dickie she began to feel bitter – who could blame her? But she pulled herself together and said to herself, "Con, you gave your life to Jesus as a girl of twelve. You're not going back now." And she never did.

When Elisabeth was only four years old she came to me one day while I was in the kitchen.

"Mummy, how do you become a Christian?"

I said, "You tell Jesus you are sorry for the naughty things you have done and ask Him to come into your heart."

"I want to be a Christian," was her response.

There and then, in the kitchen, we knelt together and in simple terms she said she was sorry for the wrong things she had done and asked Jesus to come into her life. When Bill came home she very clearly told him what had happened. He said, "That's great news, Elisabeth. I'm sure you will always try to please Jesus."

A few days after this she said to me, "Jesus came to me last night!"

I said, "That's wonderful! What happened?"

"He stood at the foot of my bed, and there was an angel with Him."

"What did Jesus and the angel look like?" I asked.

"Jesus was in white and the angel in yellow."

"Did Jesus say anything to you?"

"He said, 'Elisabeth, always do what I tell you'."

Ever since then she has sought to do just that and proved to be a very easy child to bring up. She is now a Baptist Minister.

We enjoyed our life at Whetstone. We loved the village life. One

of the new ventures was the formation of a drama group from the three churches in the village – Baptist, Congregational and Anglican. The plays all had some clear Christian message and I enjoyed acting in them. Bill did a good job at making the scenery and looking after things back stage. The wonderful thing about Whetstone was that it was a very religious village. Not in a pompous or exclusive way, but in a love for God and His world. Everyone felt they owed allegiance to one of the churches even if they only attended occasionally. There was one man, however, who clearly let it be known that he owed no allegiance to any church. Folk in the village generally referred to each other with some nickname and all referred to him as 'Rebel' and he always answered to it! There was no malice in the name and he used it of himself.

We made many lifelong friends in Whetstone. I think of Gaynor. She was a young mother with a Down's Syndrome baby. Early on in our time in Whetstone the baby died. I heard the story from Gaynor's mum who attended our church. I went to see Gaynor, feeling I could understand her through having a Down's Syndrome brother. When I met the couple Gaynor was in such a state of shock that she said nothing. The husband, I felt, seemed too glib and I was not surprised when a fortnight later he walked out. It seems he was just waiting for the baby to die.

I met her soon after and Gaynor said, "I remember when you came you said, 'adversity never leaves us as it found us. It either makes us bitter or better'."

Gaynor had taken this to heart and resolved never to become bitter. We talked and I had the joy of leading her to Jesus. She was later baptised, became a church member and, in time, a Deacon and Church Secretary. We are still friends and see each other from time to time.

Dorothy was one of the Young Wives Group. One day she had a breakdown and was unable to leave her house. On the occasions she did so she couldn't cross the road or meet with people. A group of us at Young Wives made a pact to pray for Dorothy every evening at

10.30. The Lord answered prayer and she was delivered from this breakdown.

It was a Harvest Festival day when a young lady came to the church. Glennys didn't live in Whetstone, but as she was passing through the village she felt the urge to come to the service. When the offering plate came round she had only a small coin to put in.

"I wish I had more to give to God," she thought. As she offered her coin she said in quiet prayer, "With this coin, God, I give you myself."

As she was leaving the church she talked to Mavis and Jean, two stalwart young Christians. She told them about her prayer and they said, "You must come up to the Manse and tell Glady." They brought her to me so that she might share her testimony with me. Glennys became a helper in the Girls' Club.

The ministry at Whetstone was very fulfilling in many different ways. A first ministry is not easy but the people were loving, and encouraged us in all sorts of ways. We learned in all kinds of circumstances to trust God to meet our needs.

A testing time came in an unexpected way. Once, when we were visiting our families in Edinburgh, Bill heard that Sandy, a boyhood friend of his, was in jail awaiting trial for the attempted murder of his two young children. Bill managed to get to see him in prison. He told Sandy that if he was not found guilty he could come down to us in England and we would try and help him find a new life.

Lack of appropriate evidence meant that the verdict was 'Not Proven' – a judgement that does not occur in English law. He was set free. Scottish national papers headlined the story and announced that Sandy was going off to England to start a new life. So Sandy came and the church backed up all that we sought to do for him. We got him a job and things were going well. He found acceptance in the church and our children treated him as one of the family.

Sandy was an alcoholic, but stayed off the drink until one pay day he saw an illuminated sign above a pub: 'Why not?' He went into the

pub and didn't come home. We had no idea where he was.

Christmas came and after the Christmas Day celebrations in Whetstone we went to Aylesham for a few days. When we returned, it was to find our house with a window boarded up. One of the Deacons told us how it had been discovered and the police called in. There was no other damage, but there were signs of things having been stolen. We saw the children's banks broken open and lying on the floor. We all knew who had done this. There was no bitterness towards Sandy, but there was sadness that he who had been doing so well had gone back to his old ways. When 5-year-old Mary saw her bank on the floor she said, "Look what Uncle Sandy has done! We must pray for him!" And pray for him we did. He had taken a lot of our clothes and Bill had to borrow a suit from one of the deacons to preach next day.

Sandy was eventually caught and imprisoned. Bill was allowed to speak to him after the trial, and before he was taken away to serve his sentence Bill told him we had forgiven him. Sandy thanked him for all that he and the family had done for him and said he was sorry for what he had done.

"Don't come and visit me in prison," he said to Bill. "When I get out of jail, I'll go back to Scotland." When he was released he phoned us. "I'm out of prison and I'm going back to Scotland. Thanks again for all you did for me. I'm sorry I let you and the family down." Nothing more was heard of Sandy. His family disowned him and refused to talk about him.

Some months after all this a letter came informing us that a sum of money was waiting for us in a Leicester bank. Another letter, postmarked Marlborough, Wiltshire, arrived explaining the gift.

> *Dear Mr and Mrs Rosie,*
> *You will have been advised by now of a sum of £60 to your credit at Barclays Bank. I have been led to have the sum donated to you and would wish this to be used as follows:*

£10 for books you feel you need
£15 suit or clothing for Mr Rosie
£15 dress and hat and sundries for Mrs Rosie
£20 to be spent on clothes for the children.
Please do not seek the identity of the giver, the gift has been given in the Lord's Name and I hope you will receive it in the spirit in which it is given.
Brother in Christ.

The letter was not from Sandy. We knew no one in Marlborough. The handwriting and tone of the letter suggest an elderly man. The Lord was again fulfilling His promise to provide for us. Bill wrote a letter thanking the 'brother in Christ' and asked the bank to forward it to this saint who could so clearly hear the voice of God and so readily act upon it.

After five and a half years in Whetstone Bill was called to minister in Cranham, in Essex.

It had been a great joy to serve the Lord in Whetstone and God richly blessed that time. Some years later we would come back to South Leicestershire and my calling to be a Pastor in my own right would really begin.

9

"I'll put you all in the dustbin!"

Cranham was a very different place from Whetstone. It was a new housing estate on the edge of Upminster in Essex. It was the time of the baby boom and there were lots of young families. The junior school was the largest in the country. One of the major employers was the Ford factory at Dagenham. Many travelled to work in London on the Upminster Line working in banks and insurance offices. Every morning at the same time the men would come out of their houses with briefcases and rolled umbrellas.

It made us smile to learn that our next door neighbour left for work at 8.24 each morning! By 9 o'clock they were in their offices. In the evening they came back on the same train. Saturdays they all slept later and even the milkman had to creep up the garden paths and quietly place the milk bottles on the doorsteps. Sunday was different. It was DIY day! They got up early and washed the car, painted the woodwork of the house, cut the lawns, etc. Only the people who went to church seemed to be spared this regime, but they brought their regimented approach to life into the church.

The church was only three years old and was still finding its identity and its ministry. We found that the church was well organised; in a sense it was too well organised. It was run on business lines with exact roles for various jobs. It was all right as far as it went; but they lacked the sense of being a family – which was one of the great strengths of Whetstone. Soon after we started

68

our ministry at Cranham, I went into the church kitchen where they were preparing a meal for the occasion. I expected to find the ladies busy in all sorts of ways but instead I found them lined up waiting for my arrival to delegate the various jobs! One of the first things we sought to do was to create a sense of family in the church. It took a while for them to feel easy calling us Bill and Glad, but eventually they took on board the concept of the church as the family of God and they became very caring and thoughtful towards one another.

The big regular event was the monthly Parade Sunday for the Boys' Brigade and Girls' Brigade Companies. Many considered that our Girls' Brigade Company was the best in the country! After the service there was the march round the area with the band leading the way. We developed the family service approach for these services so that all ages and not just the young could be involved. It became so popular that there was just not enough room. Every available seat would be taken. The deacons were in a little back room where they could hear but not see!

Overhead projectors were not yet available, but we developed various visual aids to help get over the message to the very wide age range. Flannelgraphs were the rage but those which were commercially produced were too small for our use, so we made our own on a larger scale. One of the church members was Fred. He was very shy but was brilliant at making things. He had a well kitted workshop and a very inventive mind. He travelled to church on a small motorbike that he built from scratch! We would have an idea for a visual aid and share it with Fred, and he would produce an expertly fashioned aid.

Quizzes were popular. Bill had the idea of a bell and buzzer quiz where two sides had to play against each other and match a question with an answer. The person who answered would come forward and push a button. The right answer was a bell tone and a wrong answer was a buzz. We wanted it to be slick and shared the idea with Fred. "Leave it with me," he said, and soon he produced a splendid large board with the questions displayed on the left and answers on the

right. At each question and answer there was a point for a probe to be placed and the idea was to match the question with the right answer. Using clever circuitry, only the correct answer would get the bell sound and all the others a buzz! It was a unique piece of equipment that helped the Parade Services to be so successful.

Another piece of equipment Fred built was like a large TV set. A large roll of paper moved between two spools like the film in a camera. I drew many pictures to appear on the screen and the whole thing was controlled remotely, placing the screen where it could best be seen. It was very effective and was in use for some years until overhead projectors became available.

When John was four and a half I was approached by the Junior School, which was next to the church, asking if I would go back to teaching. I had always felt that I should be at home for the children. When they said they would take John at the Infant School I agreed to teach mornings. John was ready for school and it worked out very well. Elisabeth was in the Junior School but she never traded on the fact that I was her mother. On one occasion she came up to me in the corridor. I was carrying some books and with a twinkle in her eye she said, "Can I carry your books, Miss?"

We encouraged fun times in the church life. We organised a Christmas party for the deacons and their spouses. This, again, was a new idea to the church. Folk got to know that we had all sorts of ideas for parties and began to ask us to organise entertainment for 21st birthday parties, silver weddings, etc.

The youth work was vibrant and a number gave their lives to Christ. We formed a link with the youth group at Mansfield run by my brother Dave and his wife Meg. We organised weekends at each others' church. A real friendship grew between the two groups. One of the events we shared together was to attend the Billy Graham meeting at Wembley Stadium. That was when we met the former Teddy Boy from Canterbury that I referred to in chapter 7.

As a church we were very involved in the Billy Graham meetings

held at Earl's Court. We took car and bus loads from the area and went every night. Bill and I were advisers working alongside the counsellors. One night Bill and I took separate cars to Earl's Court. Bill had gone on a bit earlier than the car I was in. It was the night Cliff Richard made his open confession of faith in Christ and consequently the arena and overflow was packed to capacity. When our car arrived there was no room.

"Let's go for a coffee," I suggested, "and we'll come back at the end." When we got back to the hall, Billy Graham was making his appeal for people to come forward to receive Christ. As he did so the choir sang, "The Lord's My Shepherd". I was surprised to hear the singing during the appeal, because it had been decided that there would not be the usual singing, as people had said the singing was adding an emotional element to persuade people to come forward. What we had missed was an announcement saying that there was a fire in the vicinity and the Fire Brigade had asked that the end be delayed to allow the fire engines to get to the fire. Cliff Barrows quickly got the choir to sing something they would all know – "The Lord's My Shepherd".

Some folk were leaving and so we were able to get into the hall. We could hear the choir and the familiar words, "The Lord's my Shepherd, I'll not want..." One of the ladies I had brought said, "That hymn is right. I haven't wanted the Lord to be my shepherd." She was obviously convicted by the Holy Spirit. She went forward to join the other enquirers and gave her life to Jesus. She had not heard any of the message of Billy Graham, she had apparently misunderstood the sense of the words of the hymn and yet the Holy Spirit convicted her of her need.

Now that we had a car we were able to take holidays in various parts of the country. We took a delightful holiday touring round parts of Scotland. Our first Scottish tour involved staying for a few days in Fort Augustus on the southern tip of Loch Ness. At the evening meal in the guest house where we were staying everyone

seemed somewhat quiet as they had their meal. John was about three at the time, and he decided to liven things up. He stood on his chair and shouted out, "I'll put you all in the dustbin."! In the cul-de-sac where we lived at the time the children who played together there considered this expression to be the height of naughtiness!

The children seemed to grow up fast. We encouraged them to have pets and we had quite a variety. We had a cat, a guinea pig, a budgie, and, as the children got older, we had a Shetland sheepdog. John had a couple of gerbils and every few weeks they gave birth to quite a number of baby gerbils. We wondered how to deal with these new arrivals. John showed true entrepreneurial skills by selling the offspring to the local shopkeeper! This carried on for some time until one day the pet shop owner said, "Sorry, John, I can't take any more gerbils. You've flooded the market!"

When we arrived in Cranham Mary and Ruth attended the junior school. One of the reasons why we felt it right to leave Whetstone was that we felt the standard of teaching the twins were receiving was not the standard it should be. The headmaster took the top class and, we learned later, he was suffering from an illness that meant he often fell asleep during lessons, so the children did not achieve their potential. I went to see him about the fact that the twins were not progressing in their education. He dismissed my concerns without any real discussion. "They'll never pass the 11+." I knew they were capable and I wept all the way home. It saddened us to think that Mary and Ruth should suffer adversely from our ministry in Whetstone. We prayed about the issue and the Lord indicated that for various reasons, and not just the school problem, it was time for us to move to another pastorate. Mary and Ruth went on to attend the excellent comprehensive school in Cranham. The Headteacher was a woman who had been chosen above men (no mean feat in those days) and she was determined to make her school the best it could be. Both girls succeeded in getting very good 'O' levels and were later to have very good careers. We praised God for this

wonderful provision.

We had a short prayer time together as a family in the early evening. It was a time when we had a short Bible story and would sing some songs that the children chose. I remember one occasion when John was very young and he requested, "Let's sing the song about God being on the phone."

"God is on the phone?" I asked. "I don't know that song."

"You do, you taught us it a long time ago," John said.

"Well sing it, John, and remind us what it is."

In his best singing voice John sang forth:

"God is still on the phone

And He will remember His own ..."

We all smiled! "You mean, 'God is still on the THRONE...'!" I explained his mistake to him, but said he was right about God always being there when we talk to Him.

We made some very good friends at Cranham. Jean was a young lady who felt called to overseas missionary work. This led her to train as a nurse, which involved a lot of study. There was not much room in the home she shared with her parents. It was difficult for her to get the quietness she needed to study, and we were very pleased when she asked, "Can I come and study in your house?" "Of course you can," was my reply, "but there will be one condition. You must have dinner with us and eat whatever we put in front of you!"

The reason for this condition was that we knew Jean was a very faddy eater and if she was going to be a missionary she would have to learn to eat some very strange meals. She agreed, and I had an interesting time providing all sorts of dishes. Jean later said how helpful it was. After qualifying as a nurse she went to Peru and served the Lord there for over twenty years. We are still friends and keep in touch.

Another friend was Win Dallison. She prayed her whole family into the Kingdom. One day her teenage son Graham knocked on our door on his way home from school. Unusually for that hour Bill was

73

at home and he answered the door. Graham said, "I want to become a Christian. Will you help me?" Bill gladly welcomed him in and he surrendered his life to Christ. Graham later became a Baptist Minister.

Win's husband Stan was a builder, and he came to do some work on the Manse. He was a great joker and was fun to have around. He attended church but had never made a commitment to Jesus. When he came to the Manse he noticed the seven pairs of wellingtons lined up together. As he talked to us he commented in his humorous yet serious way, "Those soles are going to Heaven. My soul isn't!" It was just at that time that we were having a mission in the church led by Frank Farley. Stan came to the meetings. One evening we could see he was struggling with the challenge. How happy we were to see him give his life to Christ. Win's prayers were certainly powerful!

Later, when we left Cranham, Mary and Ruth still had some months to go before they sat their 'O' levels. They stayed very happily with the Dallisons.

In the Autumn of 1966 I was pregnant again. Morning sickness became all day sickness and it lasted not just for the first few months but all the nine months of the pregnancy. Even when I woke up in the middle of the night I felt sick. I was teaching in the mornings and found it difficult to concentrate; but I felt I should carry on doing all that I had been doing before the pregnancy. Rose Moore, a motherly older widow and one of the deacons, helped me with some of the domestic chores. In no way did I resent the baby, for I looked forward to the new baby's arrival; but the constant sickness was difficult to cope with. After the birth I was grateful for the experience in that it helped me to understand those who had similar problems during pregnancy.

The Lord gave me a promise – "Call on Me in the day of trouble and I will deliver you." I smiled at the significance of the word 'deliver'! "Praise God," I thought, "whoever may attend me at the coming birth it will be God who will deliver the baby." The promise

gave me a great sense of contentment.

When the contractions started it was a stop and start affair and I wondered how long it would be before the labour pains started in earnest. I walked over to the tear-off calendar on the wall to reveal the date and text for the day. As I did so I asked, "Lord, how long is this going to go on?" The verse for the day was, "Six days shalt thou labour"! Who says the Lord hasn't a sense of humour! I sensed the Lord was joking with me and was gently reminding me to trust the promise He had already given me.

When the time did come there were some complications, so I had to go into hospital. However, all was well. The Lord blessed me with a lovely girl, Fiona Anne. Fiona is a Scots Gaelic name and means 'fair one'. It seemed so apt as she had fair hair and blue-grey eyes like Bill.

We had not planned another baby but we very much welcomed her coming. We called her "God's little bonus" and she was a great joy to us. This was especially so when the other children left home. She brought much happiness and I called her "my little pal". Fiona was a good baby and very easy to bring up. I was told after she was born that the umbilical cord was knotted and was twice round her neck. Fortunately, because it was long, it did not tighten and starve her of oxygen. Praise God for a safe delivery.

When six-year old John was told about the birth of Fiona he was very disappointed. "It's not fair!" he said. "I wanted twin boys!"

When I brought Fiona home, however, he soon changed. He was fascinated by this lovely little girl. He would run home from school and sit by her cot holding her hand and singing to her. He even preferred sitting with her to watching Batman, his favourite TV programme!

The ministry at Cranham was very exciting and very demanding. The congregation increased and there came the point where it was clear that we would have to extend the building to cope with all that was happening. Such was the gifting in the church that the whole

project was undertaken entirely by the church members.

The design and the construction were all carried out by the fellowship and it proved to be a great time of bonding. There was a timetable of who was doing what and when. Meals and short breaks were organised. Very important were those who provided meals and cups of tea for the manual workers. It was a very satisfying endeavour, helping to bond the fellowship together in a deep and loving way. The hall that was built was rightly referred to as the Fellowship Hall and proved to be a great asset. Some time after we left there were further extensions to the premises, but there was always a special feeling about that first extension.

Such were the pressures that there came a point when Bill felt unable to cope. Despite all I tried by way of encouragement, nothing seemed to lift the cloud. The growth in the church brought more pressure. The sense of fellowship in the church had greatly improved, but Bill often felt that his ministry was not appreciated enough. He didn't look for empty praise but for genuine appreciation. There was a crisis of confidence that only God could move. One day Bill felt that he must find an answer.

He drove to Southend to be away from the situation. The day was wet and Bill stopped the car in a car park. He asked God to speak into the situation. Bill felt God directing him to read in Isaiah. Various verses in Isaiah 43 (RSV) took on special significance. "Fear not, for I have redeemed you; I have called you by name; you are mine. You are precious in My eyes, and honoured. I love you. Remember not the former things, nor consider the things of old. Behold, I am doing a new thing." Bill's heart was lifted and he felt he could return to Cranham and that God would undertake for him.

As Bill drew near to Cranham, for no apparent reason he turned the car radio on. It was the middle of a play about two Irish brothers one of whom was a priest. The words that were being spoken, as he tuned in, were those of the brother who was not a priest. Bill heard him say, "I don't think God wants you to leave the priesthood." In a

truly remarkable way God had underlined what He had said in Southend. All doubts were gone. A breakdown had been averted.

God added a delightful postscript that evening. Bill went to put out the milk bottles at the front door before going to bed. There was a bunch of flowers laid there with a note attached. "Just a note to thank you Bill and Glad for all the help you have been to us." It was from one of the young couples in the church. How gracious of our Lord. Bill never again doubted his call to the ministry and to the pastorate at Cranham.

The time did come when God indicated to us that it was time to move. The church had grown in all sorts of areas. Most importantly they had become a family and not a business. What we were to discover was that God was going to call us to quite a different situation. There would be tremendous demands but exciting experiences of the power of the Lord.

10

"I have placed you in a large place"

When we felt it was right to move from Cranham Bill informed the Baptist Union and he was put on the list of ministers seeking a new pastorate. He received a call from the Rev Vivian Evans who had been our minister in Canterbury. He was now the Area Superintendent of the Southern Area.

"Bill, I understand you're looking for a move. I have a proposition to put to you. Can you come up to London and we can talk over a meal?"

"That all sounds very interesting," said Bill. "Hold on while I have a quick chat with Glad."

Quickly Bill shared Vivian Evans' request, and we agreed he should meet him.

"Yes, I'll come to London," said Bill.

They agreed on the venue and time. When Bill put the phone down we looked at each other wondering just what was in Vivian Evans' mind. We were both intrigued by his call. We had great respect for him and felt that it was right to hear what he had to say.

Bill met him and Vivian said, "There's a church in my area that is looking for a minister. It's a church with tremendous potential but it also has tremendous problems. When your request came for a move it came at the same time as the request from this church for a new minister. The experience you and Glad had at Aylesham

and with the Teddy Boys in Canterbury makes me think you and Glad can provide the right leadership for this church. What do you think?"

"Where is the church and what's so challenging about the situation?" asked Bill.

"It's called Leigh Park. It's a vast new housing development just outside Portsmouth. It was built to replace the housing lost in Portsmouth through the bombing in the war. There's a superb new church building built with government money given to replace a bombed out Baptist Church in Portsmouth. There are lots of social problems, but there are great opportunities for the Gospel. The previous minister has worked hard, but he felt he had to move on.

"The church is on Home Mission Grant," he continued, "and because of the difficulties in the area the Baptist Union is making a special additional payment on top of the basic stipend. Another thing you should know is that a wealthy Baptist businessman has said that he will purchase any equipment that the minister asks for to help the work. Another thing that will interest you is that Havant Grammar School is near the church."

"It sounds a tremendous challenge," said Bill. "I'll share it with Glad. We'll pray it through and let you know soon."

I had been praying very much for the meeting in London. "Well, what did Vivian Evans have to say?" I asked as soon as Bill got home. We prayed it through and decided that we had to allow Bill's name to be given to the Leigh Park Church for consideration. He was asked to come and preach. We quickly sensed that this was what God wanted for us. The church invited Bill to be the Pastor, knowing and accepting that I would have a very active role in the preaching and pastoral ministry.

One of the key points in the Lord's guidance for us were the words, "He brought me forth also into a large place" (Psalm 18:19 KJV). So strong was the guidance that I marked it in my Bible. We were reading the Psalms together at night and it amazed us to find how often the expression "a large place" (or similar) occurred. Leigh

Park was certainly a large place. It was considered to be the largest council estate in Europe! The actual church building was large. Now that we were seven we needed a large house. The church didn't have a Manse, but means were available to purchase one. We were invited to look for a house suitable for our needs. There were no houses for sale on the estate so we looked in the surrounding area. We found a three bedroom bungalow not far from the church where two additional bedrooms had been added in the loft area. Perfect! The deacons approved our choice and asked the Baptist Union surveyor to look at it. He found out that a proposed motorway was scheduled to go through the back garden!

We went down again and found a large older type house. When the surveyor looked at it he discovered that a builder had bought the house and carried out some changes. He had painted over a great deal of woodworm! That, too, had to be dismissed and we had to go down there again to try to find a suitable house. By this time some of our friends were concerned. "Are you sure you've got your guidance right?" one asked. That night the promise came again, "Thou hast set my feet in a large room." (Psalm 31:8 KJV)

A third visit was made and we found a house that had just come on the market. It was in Denvilles, an area of Havant just next to Leigh Park. It was a modern house and had four bedrooms. The largest bedroom was L shaped and the architect had originally planned that it should be divided to make a fifth bedroom. The original owners preferred it to be left as one large bedroom. This time there was no hitch. Indeed, such was the timing that as we arrived to take possession the owners came out of the door having just cleared the last of their belongings, and handed us the keys! Bill divided the large bedroom as the architect had originally planned, which meant that Fiona had her own room. Another large bedroom was partially divided so that the twins could have half each. It was virtually a six bedroom house – truly a 'large place'! There was a lovely secluded garden at the back. I felt so blessed in this house – I sat in the lounge and praised the Lord for His provision.

Why was there such difficulty in finding this house? We learned that the house in Denvilles had been put up for sale some time earlier and, because of delays in the owners' planned move to Malta, it had been taken off the market. When the way was clear for them to move to Malta it was put up for sale again. We were first on the scene so that the church could purchase this desirable property. What was frustrating for us proved to be a real blessing from the Lord. It was an important lesson for us about trusting the Lord to provide.

Leigh Park was notorious for its immorality, drug taking and violence. While we were there a murder was committed that brought TV film crews to the area. When people in the south of England asked us, "Where is your church?" and heard us answer, "Leigh Park", the usual comment was, "Oh, I am sorry for you. It must be tough!"

It **was** tough; but it was also very exciting as we saw the Lord work in great power.

Soon after arriving and getting settled in the new Manse we asked to see the Minute Book of the Church Meeting so that we could see something of what had been happening in the church in recent months. We looked at the minutes of the Church Meeting held shortly before we arrived. It had been chaired by one of the local ministers who had acted as Moderator to help the church while they sought a minister. The minutes were brief, ending with the entry, "The meeting ended in disorder"! Apparently there was discussion about the rightness of running a day nursery for young children. The church was split down the middle and so volatile were the folk on both sides that they resorted to blows! You can imagine how we felt about our future!

We had hardly begun our ministry when people from both sides asked us what we thought about the nursery the church ran.

We replied, "This is an important issue. We need to have time to see what's involved. We will see that the situation is thoroughly reviewed and discussed. There will be a special church meeting in three months' time to consider the matter."

This was accepted. For three months we preached about Christian Love. The Meeting came and it was one of the best Church Meetings we've ever shared in! The people had taken on board the teaching about experiencing and expressing *agapë* (Christian love). Apologies were given and received. The church began being a true family. The wonders God was about to perform grew out of that discovery of Christian love.

We quickly grew to love the people. Many came from difficult backgrounds. They found that Jesus didn't just patch up their lives. He transformed them! It wasn't a case of changing from 'grey' to 'paler grey' but from 'black' to 'white'! Many had known the sordid side of life and they had been dramatically changed. Because of the way God had changed them they expected God to go on working miracles. It was at the time when the charismatic renewal was affecting many Christians. The church at Leigh Park was very much at the sharp end of experiencing and expressing the gifts of the Spirit.

I have already mentioned how before we were married both Bill and I had been filled with the Holy Spirit. From time to time we had experienced the gifts of the Spirit, but to see the Holy Spirit manifest His gifts regularly in the fellowship was a new thing. At Leigh Park we saw many instances of healing.

Edith had severe asthma. One day the Lord showed me that she was ill as a result of the bitterness in her heart towards her daughter-in-law. Edith was a widow with one son. She poured out her love on this son and when he married, Edith felt the wife had stolen her son from her. Not only did she feel bitter towards the daughter-in-law, she felt bitter towards the whole family of in-laws. God not only revealed why she was ill, He also said she was not ready to receive the revelation. I must wait for the right time. Her condition worsened and she was admitted to hospital. She came out worse than when she was admitted.

Then, one day, I felt God say, "Edith is ready to receive healing. Go and see her." I shared it with Bill and we agreed that I should

obey the Lord. I went to see her while Bill prayed at home.

Edith was a very strong personality and it was with fear and trepidation I spoke to her.

"Do you know why you are ill, Edith?"

"No," she said, "I wish I did."

"You're ill, Edith, because of your bitterness towards your daughter-in-law and her family."

Her response was amazing! "You're right! I am bitter towards her, but not just her – her Mum and Grandmother ..." and so she went on, naming members of the family. God was working deeply within her. I was no longer needed. I tiptoed away. The Holy Spirit was reaching deep into her with His healing. She later apologised to all of the in-laws for the way she had treated them.

That night Edith ran out of her pills. After asking God for forgiveness she said, "Lord, be to me what these pills have been."

A few days later she kept an appointment to see the consultant. Soon after she entered the room he said to her, "I thought I was going to see Mrs Balchin; but Mrs Balchin has asthma."

"I'm Mrs Balchin," she said.

"Well, I don't know what has happened, but you have no sign of asthma now. I think you can cut down on your medication."

She told him, "I ran out of my pills a few days ago and decided I didn't need them any more."

He was amazed! She was completely healed, becoming vibrant in health and energy.

Edith became a kind of catalyst for other healings. During one of our prayer gatherings she said, "I would like you to pray for my neighbours' little boy, Simon. He's three years old and has cancerous growths like black grapes in the crook of his arms and between his nose and upper lip. The surgeon said he could do nothing for him. The best advice he could give was, 'Have another child'."

We prayed for him. A fortnight later when Bill was in his study at church Edith knocked on the door. "Bill, I've brought Simon to see you." In came Simon. The growth under his lip was flesh coloured

and had almost disappeared. There were what looked like freckles in the crook of his arms! Simon was wonderfully healed. Not long after, Simon's mother had a baby – not as a replacement for Simon but as a little sister.

During another Thursday Prayer Meeting Edith said, "Please pray for Mr Rope, a neighbour of mine." Edith lived in a tower block and she seemed to be neighbour to them all. "Mr Rope lives alone. He has lung cancer and it seems to be rather advanced."

We prayed for him. On the Saturday Bill took him into hospital where he was to have surgery, and Edith came with him. They stayed with Mr Rope until he was called to go for X-rays in preparation for the operation. Bill said to him, "Would you like me to pray for you?"

"Yes please," he answered. "I've never had anyone pray for me before. I don't really believe in God but, by all means, pray for me."

Bill gave a short prayer for him and they left him as he entered the lift taking him to the X-ray department.

Edith went to visit Mr Rope on the Sunday afternoon. She expected to see him in bed and was surprised to see him sitting by his bed fully clothed.

"Why are you sitting out of bed?" she asked. "I expected to see you in bed getting some kind of pre-operation care ready for your operation tomorrow."

"I'm not having an operation tomorrow! When you left me to go for an X-ray they found the cancer had shrunk! They showed me the X-ray that first showed the cancer and other subsequent X-rays that showed its growth. The one they took yesterday showed a dramatic change. It was much reduced! The surgeon said to me, 'I can't understand it. You're a very lucky man, Mr Rope. We'll postpone the operation and see what happens.' They're sending me home tomorrow."

Soon the cancer was completely gone and Mr Roper believed in God as a result of his experience.

One Sunday evening we had had an informal fellowship meeting in a house, and as people were beginning to leave Edith mentioned

that her sister had breast cancer and was in hospital in Gloucester. We prayed for her sister and for Edith. One of the deacons said, "I've been reminded of how it mentions in the Bible that Paul sent handkerchiefs to people they prayed for. We can't go to Edith's sister. Have you got a clean handkerchief, Edith?" She had, and we prayed over it and asked that it would be a point of contact for her sister with us.

Edith sent it and we learned that a nurse pinned it to Edith's sister's nightdress. There were seven cancers and soon six of them had disappeared!

The surgeon came to her and said, "You have been too ill for us to operate, but you're a lot stronger now and I could operate on the remaining deepest cancer."

"No thank you," she said. "If God can heal the six then He can heal the seventh."

"I wish others had faith like yours," said the surgeon.

And God **did** heal the seventh.

As well as seeing healings, and there were others, we experienced other gifts of the Spirit. Bill and I had never spoken in tongues before we came to Leigh Park. We had experienced other gifts but we never spoke in tongues. We had been present in gatherings where tongues were manifested, but so often it didn't seem to ring genuine. We longed to experience all that God had for us and we felt that He would give us the gift of tongues in His own good time.

During an after-service home meeting on a Sunday evening, Sir Tom Lees and his wife Faith spoke. Here were a couple as far removed from traditional Pentecostalism as you could imagine. They spoke of the filling of the Holy Spirit and speaking in tongues, and asked if anyone would like them to lay hands on them and pray for the gift of tongues. Bill received this gift that evening as Tom Lees laid hands on him. Though I was prayed for it didn't happen for me that night. It was several months of waiting and praying and weeping before I first sang and then prayed in tongues at a Fountain

Trust Conference.

Present at that meeting where Tom Lees spoke was a young man who had recently started attending our church. He had been in a serious car accident and had suffered some brain damage. This affected his speech which was very slurred and indistinct. He asked for prayer, and he then spoke with great eloquence in an unknown tongue! It was quite an amazing experience and began a healing process in his speaking.

One Sunday morning we were waiting for our organist to arrive. Shortly before the service was due to start we had a message from him to say that he would not be able to come. His young son had been stung by a wasp and was having a severe reaction. Another member took his place. At the start of the service Bill told the congregation and prayers were offered asking for the boy's healing. There was a wonderful sense of the Lord's Presence and power. Bill had a word of knowledge that the boy was healed and he was so convinced it was from the Lord that he said to the congregation, "The Lord has answered our prayers. The boy is healed! Hallelujah!"

We heard later that while we were all praying the boy turned to his mother and said, "Mummy, Jesus has made me better!"

During our time at Leigh Park, Edna Evans (Vivian's wife) often asked me to speak at Ministers' Wives' conferences. I had often spoken at Women's Rallies and when I was at Aylesham I spoke at a Women's Rally in Canterbury Cathedral. Being a woman I was not allowed to speak from the pulpit since at that time the Anglican Church did not accept women in ministry. I spoke from the Chancel steps. I was often asked to counsel women and felt it was a strong part of my ministry, leaving the counselling of men to Bill.

There were many demands made upon us and we were glad when one particular married couple started attending the church. They had experience of the charismatic renewal and we felt they would be a great help in maturing the people in the things of the Spirit. All had gone well for a time and then the services seemed to go spiritually

flat. The dynamic had gone. The Deacons became remote from us. Joy had gone out of the worship. We prayed and wondered what to do. There were no other churches or ministers near to help us because we were the 'front runners' in the area regarding the charismatic renewal. This couple asked us to go and see them, and we felt that perhaps they could help solve the problem.

We went to see them and shared with them how we felt. They agreed that the worship was sterile and came to the conclusion that we should move to another church!

The suggestion was painful. It was made worse when they suggested that the reason the Lord had sent them to the church was so that they could lead it forward in the things of the Spirit. We left their house feeling very low. "Lord, what is Your will?" was the cry of our hearts.

As we sought the Lord He made it very clear. They were messengers of Satan! We cried to the Lord, "Move them or change them!" The Lord moved them. Very soon after our meeting with them they left the area. As we shared this with the Deacons, it became clear that this couple had been trying to influence them and draw them away from us. The Deacons said they were sorry for allowing this couple to influence them. Together we reaffirmed the Lordship of Jesus among us. This was reaffirmed as the Deacons prayed with us before the start of the next service. Many said after the service, "Your faces shone as you came out of the vestry." The blessing was restored and a valuable lesson learned.

The children were growing up quickly. Mary started teacher training at Eastbourne. Ruth attended Secretarial College. Liz was doing well at Havant Grammar School. John was attending Denvilles Junior School and was working towards his 11+. Fiona was approaching the time when she would start school. Sadly, there came the time when John became ill. The doctors found difficulty in diagnosing his illness which caused depression and a skin complaint. He was given a brain scan to see if he was epileptic, but this was

inconclusive. For a year we battled under a cloud.

The church continued to move forward, but at home we were all too aware of what John was going through. His school work began to suffer. His flair for writing and illustrating stories ceased. We battled on and God wonderfully supported us. There came a time when some close friends of ours who didn't come to our church mentioned that an American evangelist they knew called Dick Carter was going to be passing through Portsmouth on his way to France. They felt he had the type of ministry that could help John.

"He can call for a couple of hours before he has to go to the ferry," they said. "Do you want him to come?"

We were prepared to try almost anything to help John and we respected the spiritual insights of this couple. "Yes, please ask him to call."

This couple came to our house to be with us when Dick Carter came. It was midday when the evangelist and his son zoomed into our drive on their high-powered motorbikes. He quickly made himself at home and listened to our story as we shared lunch. We joined hands together and waited for the Lord to minister. There were no histrionics. Everything was quiet, but there was a very real sense of the Presence of the Lord. He prayed that the house would have a new sense of God's peace. He prayed for John to be healed and restored to his former healthy state. We had a deep sense that the Lord was present and had answered the prayer to restore John.

Dick Carter then prayed for us in a way we had not expected. The Lord gave him a word for me and for Bill. He said, "Glad, God has given you the gift of wisdom that will help many in their relationship with the Lord. Bill, you will have a wider ministry than you have had until now." Dick Carter said that there might be signs of a relapse with John. "If it happens, reject it in the Name of the Lord. God has healed John. Hold on to that."

It was time to leave and these two 'Heaven's Angels' zoomed off on their powerful machines to make their way to the Continent of Europe.

John did get better. His skin healed up wonderfully. There was one brief relapse which was soon dispelled by prayer. John got back his enthusiasm for school and was successful in his 11+ exam. He now had to wear glasses, but that just helped to make him look like Joe 90, one of the well-known TV characters at the time. A new and deeper peace filled the house. And we wondered about the significance of what Dick Carter had said about us.

During the time of John's illness we still experienced blessing in the church. People were coming to know Christ and were being baptised and becoming church members. I remember at the end of one baptismal service Bill said, "If God has spoken to you and you want to do something about it then come forward for prayer. Is He calling you to be baptised? Is there something you need to put right in your life and you want help? Come forward and someone will pray with you."

There was quietness and then I heard a tapping sound and wondered what it was. I opened my eyes and there was Doris struggling down the aisle with the help of her walking stick. Doris had MS and walking was a struggle. I went up to her. "Why have you come forward, Doris?" I expected her to say, "I want prayer for my MS." I was surprised when she said, "I want to be baptised."

I was both surprised and thrilled. Surprised because of her illness and the practical problems it would cause for baptism, yet thrilled at her readiness to obey the Lord. I prayed with her. Later, Bill and I discussed the baptism with her. It was decided that it was not practical to attempt to baptise her by total immersion. It was decided that, since she could get into the baptistry with help, Bill would pour water over her. A date was fixed for her baptism.

On the Wednesday night before her baptism Doris woke up in the night. She felt God speak to her in a very definite way. "Doris, I'm going to heal you." It seemed so natural that she just said, "All right Lord, thank You." She turned over in bed and went to sleep. She told us about it and it was agreed that Bill would link prayer for

healing with the act of baptism. Sunday came. Bill told the congregation that he would be praying for Doris's healing and asked them to be praying also. Everything was set for the baptism. Doris was helped into the baptistry. Bill poured the water over her and prayed for her healing. Others joined in the prayer. Doris walked out of the baptistry! She walked home without the need for her stick! She went shopping next day, again without her stick! It was amazing. Doris said that for the first time in years she was aware of feeling in her feet as she stood in the baptistry.

Doris was not completely healed at that point. In stages certain areas affected by the MS were healed. She continued to attend her MS self-help group. Others in the group noticed how Doris was getting better. One day one of the people in the group said, "Doris, you're looking great and you're obviously getting better. What pill are you on?" In a flash Doris replied, "The 'Gospill'!" She shared with them how God was working in her life.

One of our members rang us one day. "Can you come over? I need help for Frank."

"What's the problem?" I asked.

"Come over and we'll tell you."

We dropped what we were doing and went to the house. Frank and his wife were waiting for us. Frank was a gentle, caring person. He never looked particularly well but never grumbled. He had been a nurse, but was now unemployed. They had a young daughter who was not there when we arrived.

"What's the matter?" I asked.

Frank told us his story. He trained as a nurse and had access to drugs. One time when he was under stress he took some drugs. He found himself doing it more and more. He was discovered and dismissed. The craving continued. He got further access to drugs and often became unconscious. Once he fell into the fire and was badly burned. Now he wanted to be free from his addiction.

"Please help me. I can't cope and the family are suffering."

We both felt a deep compassion for Frank. Knowing Bill would back me up I said, "Frank, God can help you and He will if you really are determined to come off the drugs. Come and stay with us for a while so that the family can have some respite. It won't be easy for you, but being in another environment will help. Bill and I will be on hand to help you."

Frank and his wife agreed. He packed a small case and came with us. We now had to work out what to do!

It was important that Frank was never left alone. Bill slept in the same room with Frank. Whenever Frank craved for drugs we dropped what we were doing and prayed with him. Always the Lord gave strength to Frank. If craving came in the night, Bill would pray and God would answer. The next Sunday we had a special speaker, one of the Sisters of Darmstadt in Germany. She shared the wonderful story of God's grace and power through this Protestant Convent in Germany. The service was followed by ministry for any who wanted it. Frank was sitting next to me. I wondered if he would go forward for prayer. He turned to me, "I want to go home."

"Home?" I asked. "What home do you mean?"

"Your home."

Bill had to stay at church and I took Frank home. He was very agitated. I turned on the TV to help him think of something else. I made some strong coffee and prayed inwardly that God would help him through.

"I need to go back home."

"Why?" I asked.

"I need to get rid of the drugs I've got in the house." "Praise the Lord," I thought. "This is a real breakthrough."

"We'll go over tomorrow and see to it," I said.

Next day we took Frank to his home. He rooted out his drugs and he and Bill flushed them all down the toilet. He spent some time with his wife and then came back with us to our home.

Our friend Heather from Aylesham was with us for a few days and she was a great help in prayer for Frank. The heart of our praying was that the Holy Spirit would take the place of the drugs and be the

stimulation for his life. After only a fortnight we all felt that Frank could go back home. He looked healthier than we had ever known him. He had found a new faith in the Lord and the power of the Holy Spirit. His wife and daughter were thrilled to have him home, a new man. Some time later Frank got work in an organisation helping drug addicts. His own experience and his deep faith were now wonderfully used by the Lord.

There is one more incident that I want to relate. The phone rang about midnight. It was Joan, one of the young wives at church. She was crying and in obvious distress.

"Please come and help me. Bernard has gone berserk. He's been hitting me. I've managed to get out of the house and I'm ringing from a phone box. Please help me."

"Where is Bernard now?" asked Bill.

"I saw him leave the house. I don't know where he is."

"Are the children all right?"

"Yes, they're in bed."

"Go back to the house," said Bill, "lock the door and I'll come over right away."

Within minutes Bill was there and she let him in. She was very distressed. Bill prayed the Lord's peace into the situation and she told her story. "From time to time during our marriage Bernard has had bouts of physical and sexual violence. Suddenly it would flare up and as quickly subside. I've never shared it with anyone else, only my mother and she vowed to keep it a secret. However, I feel he has gone too far. He could have killed me tonight. I don't want to involve the police but I wonder what he'll do to the children." Bill prayed with her and she became more relaxed. "Go to bed. I'll wait here. I'm sure Bernard will come back when he's quietened down."

Eventually Bernard returned. If he was surprised to see Bill he didn't show it. He sat down and was obviously very shaken as a result of what had happened.

"Bernard, what's got into you? Joan has told me what's happened

tonight," said Bill. "She's very frightened and upset. This can't go on."

Bernard spoke with difficulty, finding it hard to express himself. "I don't know what happened. Suddenly I just started to feel violent. There was no reason for it."

Bill didn't tell him Joan had mentioned other incidents. He asked, "Has it happened before?"

"Yes, there have been a number of times when, for no apparent reason, I've become violent. Poor Joan, the things I've done to her. In spite of what I've done, I do love her."

"Try and describe what causes you to be violent," said Bill.

"It all happens without warning. It's as though some power overwhelms me and I'm powerless to keep it at bay."

"What do you think that 'power' can be?"

"I'm almost afraid to admit it but I think it's some evil power that overcomes me."

"When did you first begin to feel like this?"

"I've always had problems with sudden bouts of temper. When I became a Christian it seemed to go away, but after a while it came back with a vengeance." Bill felt that the Lord made the cause clear, but he was hesitant to suggest it.

He said, "You're right, Bernard, that some evil power is responsible. I believe that from childhood an evil spirit has affected you. Lately, he has become more open and more violent because of what's happening in the church. He wants to discredit the work of God at Leigh Park. Do you want to be rid of this evil spirit?"

"Yes I do," he quickly replied.

"Are you prepared to open up your life afresh to God to be filled with the Holy Spirit rather than this evil spirit?"

"Yes."

Very simply and with no histrionics Bill prayed, "In the Name of Jesus and by the power of the Holy Spirit I command you spirit of violence and lust to leave this child of God. Leave him and go to the place God has prepared for you. Holy Spirit, come and fill Bernard

with Your love and grace. Enable him to start again as a husband to Joan and a father to the children. In the Name of Jesus. AMEN."

Bill saw an immediate change in Bernard and told him to go upstairs and share with Joan what had happened. He went up to their bedroom. Bill waited a while and sensed that it was safe to leave.

There is an interesting postscript to this incident. Five years later, which was four years after we left the ministry at Leigh Park, Joan had cause to write us a letter. At the end of the letter she said, "You'll be pleased to know that there has been no trouble with Bernard since that day Bill prayed for him." Praise the Lord for His work of grace!

I want to emphasise that all that was achieved at Leigh Park was in and through the Holy Spirit. Various individuals were used in all sorts of wonderful ways. It was significant that no one person was at the centre. It was very much a case of the church being responsive to the Holy Spirit. Many had their stories to tell of how the Holy Spirit used them in leading others to Christ and how the Spirit equipped them through His gifts and graces. The people learned to listen to God and act upon His guidance.

One of the agencies God was using to bless many churches at this time was 'One Step Forward'. The purpose of OSF, as many called it, was to encourage healthy church life and thereby to see church growth. It had started in a simple way in Essex when three Baptist ministers shared ideas and came up with a simple programme to help churches grow in health and numbers. A number of churches benefited from this and our church at Cranham had been one of the first to use this programme and benefit from its teaching. One of the three Baptist ministers, Bryan Gilbert, felt called to leave the pastorate and go full time into this ministry in order to respond to the requests for the programme. Many sought the ministry of Bryan and in Europe and the USA there were requests for him to promote and help churches use the OSF programme. Bryan asked Bill if he would consider joining him in OSF as the UK Director, to enable him

to concentrate on the overseas request.

We wondered what to do about this request. We felt very strongly that our ministry was the pastoral ministry in the local church and yet there was something about this request we could not ignore. We remembered the word of prophecy to Bill when Dick Carter came and prayed regarding John, "Bill, you will have a wider ministry." Is this what God wanted for us? We shared this with some trusted friends and the word became clear: Bill would join Bryan. He would do so for three years to help Bryan deal with the overseas requests and then return to the pastoral ministry. The church was sad when it was shared with them. The Deacons prayed things through and agreed that this call was from the Lord. There was personal sadness but they had so tasted the work of the Holy Spirit that they knew they could trust the Lord to provide for them.

An interesting point about the call to One Step Forward is that the base was in South Leicestershire in a village near Whetstone, our first church! Bryan now lived in Whetstone and he was a member there. One of those we shared with regarding working in OSF was Ron, who was treasurer of OSF and a member at Whetstone from our time there. His advice and assistance was very helpful to us in reaching our decision. It is interesting to see that our two previous churches, Whetstone and Cranham, had a part to play in this call to join One Step Forward.

11

"You can get central heating or a garage, but not both"

The move to South Leicestershire meant that we had to find a house. The first thing we had to do was find out what price of house we could get. We found that we could get a mortgage for £5,000. What kind of house could we get for that money in 1972?

We asked our friends Ron and Flo from Whetstone to look around for us and tell us what we could get within our budget. Ruth would not be moving with us because she was soon to marry and would stay in the Leigh Park area. Mary was at College but would need a room to come home to. Our friends got all the information they could and got in touch with us.

"House prices are beginning to increase in this area. The best you can expect to get is a three-bedroom house with central heating or a garage, but not both." "OK," we said, "see what you can find and let us know." Soon they found a house with three bedrooms, central heating *and* a garage! "We'll come up right away."

It meant a bit of reorganising our commitments but we drove up to Leicestershire. We were so thrilled to get both central heating and a garage that we quickly said, "We'll have it!" We rejoiced that the housing situation was solved so quickly. But our joy was short-lived. The phone rang. "Hi, Glad. It's Flo here. I've got some bad news for you. Another buyer has offered a high price for the house and the owners have accepted."

We couldn't go higher, so there was nothing we could do. It was back to square one.

Why had this setback happened? We realised that we hadn't really prayed about that house. We relied on the circumstances as all the guidance we needed. We learned our lesson; we prayed for forgiveness and a greater sensitivity to discern the Lord's will. I remember saying to Bill, "I think this setback means that God has something better for us and more suited to our needs."

We rang Ron and Flo and said, "A four-bedroom house would be better suited to our needs!" "That would be a miracle! We'll keep looking."

One Sunday afternoon Flo rang, "We've found a two-bedroom bungalow where the roof has been opened up to create two more bedrooms – four bedrooms! And it has central heating and a garage! When can you come and see it?"

We had a quick chat and agreed that we needed to act quickly. "If it's all right for us to stay with you we can come up tonight after the evening service and view it tomorrow."

"Great," said Flo. "It will be lovely to have you stay with us. I'll ring the present owners and fix a time for tomorrow morning. Have a good journey."

We saw the house next morning. It was in Fleckney, a village in South Leicestershire we knew well from our time in Whetstone. We were delighted; but learning from our previous experience, we realised that we must get a sure word from God. We said to the owners, "We like the house very much. It's well suited for our needs, but we are Christians and we want to pray about it first. We'll go back to our friends' house and come back this afternoon and let you know our decision."

They said, "That's fine. We'll hold it for you and look forward to seeing you this afternoon."

We had lunch with Flo and then she left us to pray through the situation. We prayed for a sure word from God about the house. We each read as we felt led by the Lord and looked for Him to give us the same guidance. When we both felt that we had a word from the Lord

we shared what we had found. Bill was led to read in Joshua 14. When he read, "Forty years old was I when... sent... to espy out the land" (Josh 14:6) Bill began to feel the passage was particularly significant, because he himself was forty years old. Then the words, "surely the land whereon thy feet have trodden shall be thine inheritance" seemed to speak into the situation. I felt led to read 2 Chronicles 20:9, "We stand before this house... for Thy Name is in this house". Normally we would not advocate such random reading of the Scriptures for guidance, but there was such a limited time. The two readings so backed each other up and we felt so agreed within ourselves that we felt that the Lord was clearly leading us to buy this property. We went back to the house. When we told the couple we wanted to buy it, they said, "We thought you would. And knowing you're pushed for time we've measured the windows for you." The purchase of the house in Fleckney proved ideal for our needs – four bedrooms, central heating and a garage!

Fleckney was a village much like Whetstone. The people were friendly and welcoming. An incident happened just a few weeks after we arrived there that will give some idea of the friendliness of the village. A friend of ours was passing through the village and he thought he would call on us. He didn't know Fleckney and couldn't find our street. He asked one of the locals, "Could you tell me where Kilby Road is please?" The local replied, "Who are you looking for?" "Bill and Glad Rosie, they've just recently moved here." Our friend was given directions and then the villager said, "There's no point in calling. They're not in."! Our friend laughed when he later rang us and told us about this example of village friendliness.

People had been saying to me, "You and Bill have always worked together in churches. What are you going to do now? You can't travel with him. You still have Fiona (four), John (ten) and Liz (fifteen) at home."

"I will, of course, stay at home, but I'm sure the Lord will have some work for me to do that doesn't interfere with looking after the children."

I was perfectly content, and before we left Leigh Park to move to Fleckney the Lord revealed His particular plan for me.

Because we were known in South Leicestershire, the East Midlands Area Superintendent wrote to us when he heard that Bill was joining One Step Forward. He asked us if we would consider pastoring village churches in South Leicestershire. Bill would not have any time to undertake such a request, but it very much appealed to me. I would have time during the day when the children were at school to do this pastoring. I offered my readiness to pastor the two churches of Arnesby and Walton. Both these churches were near Fleckney, where the house was that God had chosen for us. After the churches and I had met, they both called me unanimously to be their lay Pastor. Now I would exercise pastoral ministry purely in my own right and not just as Bill's wife. This wonderful provision by God excited us both.

There is a lovely postscript to our ministry at Leigh Park. Shortly before we left, Annette, a lovely elderly lady, came to see us. She had followed the Lord for many years and was a great encouragement to us.

"Thank you for your ministry and your friendship," she said. "The Lord has told me to give this to you, Glad. Now that Bill will be travelling a lot you will need a car of your own to do the work God wants you to do. I have money enough to meet my needs. It's a privilege to feel that I can be of help to you in your work for the Lord."

It was a cheque large enough to buy a good second-hand car!

I accepted a part-time teaching post at a local village school where Fiona would be going, but I knew I could fit in this other commitment also. It was a very happy school with only twenty-one pupils. The headmistress took the seniors and I took the juniors. We only had one big room and most of the teaching was individual. It was a big happy family and there were no discipline problems. The

headmistress's husband was very amused to know I was a Pastor. He had never met a woman Minister and when he saw me on sports day in trousers, he came to me and whimsically enquired, "Have you been defrocked?"

Arnesby was a very old Baptist church dating back to the 17th century. One of the first things I did was to start a Girls' Club for girls of seven and over. One of the ladies from the church helped me and so did our daughter Liz. There were varied activities including games, hobbies and refreshments, but there was always a spiritual element. One by one the girls came to know Jesus personally. Many came to know Christ through the annual camp that we held. Such was the popularity of the club that before very long every girl in the village between seven and fourteen belonged to it. They began inviting their friends from the neighbouring village of Shearsby, and soon all the girls from there belonged as well. Liz taught a group of the girls to play the guitar and we formed a ministry team which was often asked to share in children's meetings in other churches.

A Bible study group was started and it was a joy one night to hear an old lady pray whom I hadn't heard do so before. I visited her that week. I said to her, "It was lovely hearing you share in prayer at our last meeting. Have you ever prayed in public before?" "Oh yes," she replied. "I used to do so when I attended Christian Endeavour." "How long ago was that?" I asked. "Oh, it must be fifty years ago," was her reply!

Walton was even smaller than Arnesby. It was a farming community and everything arranged at church had to fit in with milking the cows. I started a home meeting and we met in the different farms of the members. Being such a rural community the Harvest Festival was an important occasion and was very much a real thanksgiving for the produce of the land. I became very know-ledgeable about farming as I visited the people.

One damp and foggy November evening, as I was driving out to one of the Walton farms to lead a Bible Study, two figures loomed out of the darkness. They were thumbing a lift and I stopped.

"Could you give us a lift to our caravan, please?" they asked.

"Of course, hop in."

I later learned that their names were Dave and Marina. They fetched a pram that was by the hedge.

"Sorry," I said, "I can't possibly take the pram."

"We'll leave it here and come back for it tomorrow."

Dave bent into the pram and produced some articles and a dog! We set off and after a while Dave said, "Turn left here into this farm road." We came to a rough track. "Follow this track." The track became a field and in a corner was their caravan. There was no heating and no lighting. They had no food. I quickly realised how desperate their situation was and said, "I have to get to my meeting but I'll be back tomorrow." My car was stuck in the mud and Dave ran to the farm for help. To my relief the farmer was willing and able to use his tractor to get me moving.

I arrived at the farmhouse where the house meeting was being held. I explained the reason for being late. "I'm sure God wants us to help this couple," I said, and everyone agreed. Next day I went round the various homes of the group. I collected food, clothing, blankets, an offer of a bath, and so on. Dave and Marina started coming to church. They started to get something of a life together. Dave got a job and they managed to get an old car. Sadly, however, Dave was arrested for driving the car without a licence. Marina was expecting a baby and was moved to a hostel. We had helped them all we could. They left the area and we lost touch with them; but we thank God for the opportunity to help them.

While we were living at Fleckney, Ruth married Ceilig, who was one of the young men who attended Leigh Park. It was lovely going back to Leigh Park for the wedding. Ruth was secretary to Ceilig's father and they set up their first home in the family house. When Mary finished her teacher training she married Kevin, who lived in Portsmouth and again it was another wedding down south. Kevin came from a strongly Catholic family and they were married in a Catholic church. After Mary left College she started teaching in outer

London and so they set up home near Epping Forest.

Since we had our own house at Fleckney, the Manse at Arnesby was not being used. It was decided to turn the Manse into a small conference centre, making part of it into a flat for a warden, and leaving other rooms and some church rooms to accommodate groups for their various activities. With minor alterations to the manse and church this was done and all that remained was to find someone to act as warden. Ruth and Ceilig were finding it difficult sharing the house of Ceilig's parents and it was felt right by those concerned with the appointment of the warden that they should be approached to consider becoming wardens at Arnesby. The idea was put to them and they agreed to be the first wardens at the Arnesby Christian Conference Centre. Soon groups of all ages were coming for weekends and longer. It was a joy, too, having Ruth and Ceilig living near us.

In the summer months Bill led a particular kind of ministry to village churches in different parts of the country. Young people, mostly students, with some coming from Europe, offered their time to help mainly rural churches. There was always an evangelistic emphasis in this work. The groups were referred to as Action Teams and were among the first, if not the first, to encourage students to give help to small churches and at the same time learn about evangelism. Liz shared in some of these Action Teams.

Liz was going out with Sean, a brother of Ceilig. One weekend, while Liz was with Bill on one of the Action Teams, I was helping to run a fête on the Saturday at Arnesby. Sean was there and he said to me, "Glady, with Bill and Liz away would you like to come out for a meal tonight? We could make a foursome with Ruth and Ceilig." I had a sermon to prepare for the next day but I felt God was saying this invitation was important.

"That would be great," I replied, "but I have a sermon to prepare. Would it be too late to call for me about 8 o'clock?"

"That'll be great."

After the meal I invited the three of them back for coffee. As we relaxed together at home we started talking about God, and Sean became somewhat argumentative. Everything was in good humour but I sensed that Sean was seeking for God but that he was reticent to say so openly.

I said, "Why not come to Walton next Saturday. We're having a bonfire. Bill and Liz and the Action Team will be there. You'll enjoy meeting the Action Team. They're a great bunch. You'll particularly like to meet Bryan Adams, one of the Team."

"Is that the Bryan Adams who has been chosen to walk in the Olympic Games?"

"Yes. You'll enjoy meeting him. Bryan Gilbert will also be there and he's going to give a talk."

"What, in the open air?" Sean asked. He thought preaching was only done in church buildings.

"Yes. There will be nothing stiff and starchy about it."

Sean came to the bonfire and afterwards had a chat with Bryan Gilbert. The Action Team took the service the following Sunday evening at Walton. Sean came. Bill led the service and Bryan Gilbert spoke. After the service Bill could sense that God was challenging Sean. Bill said simply to him, "Do what you have to do." Sean went for a walk by himself, dealing with the implications of what God was saying to him. He came back. The decision had been made. He had given his life to Christ.

What none of us knew was that while Liz was away with the Action Team she had prayed, "Lord, if Sean hasn't become a Christian within a fortnight, I'll stop going out with him." I had the joy of baptising Sean some time later. He and Liz married in the Arnesby Church and they bought a house in Fleckney.

While we were living at Fleckney the Baptist Union introduced the idea of Supplementary Ministry. The idea was that people would study up to the usual standard of ministers at college and then become part of a team. It was understood that they would not

receive a stipend but have independent means. I thought this seemed appropriate for me, so I began my studies and was given a tutor in Loughborough. This meant that I had a very heavy schedule of work. I got up very early in the morning to study. After breakfast, Fiona and I would go the school at Kilby. I shopped in the dinner hour, did pastoral visiting in the afternoon, met Fiona coming out of school and got home to get the tea ready. Often there were meetings in the evening and I would leave Liz in charge of things.

There was a One Step Forward meeting just outside Leicester. Bryan was speaking. I went and seven-year-old Fiona came with me. When Bryan made an appeal for people to stand in their places if they wished to receive Christ, Fiona was the first to stand. It was something she did of her own volition. She was in the front row and was completely unaware of any response from people behind her. It was a very meaningful response that thrilled us both.

Bryan said, "A little child shall lead them."

Bill was away a lot taking meetings in various parts of the country and for different denominations. It meant that he became very aware of the spiritual state of the nation at that time. He did, however, manage to be at home for a good number of weekends. It was decided that he would become a member at Fleckney Baptist Church and so leave me free to pursue my own ministry. John went with Bill and Fiona came with me. Fiona was a real 'little pal' and we enjoyed doing things together. She would often be my passenger in the car and she quickly learned how to read maps and be aware of traffic situations. From a very early age she learned to say at junctions, "All right on the left!"

The number of children at school grew. One day the Head Teacher said to me, "We've grown so much in size that I need another full-time teacher. Could you come full time, Glad? It would be great if you could."

I had to say, "No, I'm sorry, I can't. Much as I love the work, and the children, I feel I can't work full time. Thanks for asking me."

Another teacher was appointed, but I will always have a soft spot for the delightful infant school at Kilby.

I got another part-time teaching post at a larger village school in Husbands Bosworth. I had a small class of just seven children but it was no ordinary group of children.

"The class is small," said the headteacher, "because each of them has some kind of learning difficulty that makes it difficult for them in the ordinary class situation. I feel they will gain from being in this small group in the mornings and in the larger classes in the afternoon."

It was a challenge, but I felt right about accepting the post.

"Make your own syllabus. I'll give you all the support you need."

The children were all very needy in different ways – dyslexic, hyperactive, emotionally deprived, and so on. I prayed very much that the Lord would give me love and wisdom for these children.

Probably the most difficult child was Jane. She was hyperactive and very rebellious. One morning she was particularly naughty. When playtime came I drew her aside and said to her, "Jane, do you like being naughty?" "No," she said, "but I can't help it."

It was a Church school so I felt it was quite in order to say to her, "Let's tell Jesus about it." I gave a simple prayer, "Jesus, help Jane not to be so naughty." Very quickly after that I saw a huge improvement in her behaviour and, consequently her ability to learn. The Head came to me. "We've seen a tremendous improvement in Jane. She can come back into the ordinary classroom situation after Christmas."

We had very good neighbours, Ted, Sheila and their teenage son. Ted was rather shy and had a speech impediment. Sheila had health problems, the main one being arthritis. Fairly soon after we arrived in Fleckney Ted asked me, "Do you play canasta?"

"No," I said.

"Would you like to learn?"

We like playing all sorts of games, so I said, "Yes, that would be lovely." So we arranged a time when Bill was home and learned how to play canasta. In time Ted began to open up to us. He knew we

were Christians and was aware of the Bible Study group that met in our house.

"I used to be a preacher," he said when he got to know us better. "But I lost my faith. It didn't seem to work for me."

We shared with him how we felt sure that the Lord understood all the problems he had and that he could find a new faith that could transform his life.

"Can I start again? Will Jesus forgive me for turning my back on Him?"

"Most certainly," we assured him.

Eventually all three gave their lives to Jesus. Remarkably, although Ted stuttered in ordinary conversation, when he prayed aloud in our house meetings he spoke with great fluency.

One morning Ted knocked on the door just before he went to work. "Could you look in on Sheila today, Glady? I've left her some sandwiches and a drink, but the arthritis is so bad she can't reach out to feed herself." "Of course I will. I'll pop in shortly and see how she is." I found Sheila lying in her bed, too stiff to move and unable to sit up. I felt the Lord giving me a special love for her.

As we spoke I felt it right to say to her, "Would you like me to pray for you, Sheila?"

"Yes, please," she answered.

"Where is the main root of your arthritis?" I asked.

"It's my back. It's so painful I can't even turn over in bed or sit up."

"Would you mind if I turned you round so that I could lay my hands on your back and pray that the Lord will heal you?"

"Oh please do, but I don't know if I'll be able to turn to let you touch my back."

With great difficulty, for she was a large woman, I managed to turn her so that she lay on her front. Gently I ran my hands up and down her back. "Lord, heal Sheila. Take away the pain. Take away the rigidity. Bring new health to enable Sheila to get up and walk around with freedom."

It was all very quiet but there was a wonderful sense of the Lord being present and bringing healing.

There was no immediate change. I helped her with her meal and then left. Next morning Ted came to our door to tell us how God had touched Sheila. She was a changed woman! The Lord had wonderfully touched her body. She was able to move about free of pain. She had got the meal ready for Ted when he returned from work. It was a remarkable healing from the Lord. It was an added indication that the Lord had brought us to that particular house so that she and the whole family could find Him.

Bill had known all along that one day he would go back into the pastorate. He had promised Bryan that he would give three years to One Step Forward. He had done more than that as the work developed in all sorts of ways. He enjoyed the different kind of ministry that OSF made possible, but his heart was in local church ministry. It was all very well being the 'special speaker' on many occasions. It was good being able to help churches grow spiritually and numerically. The work with the Action Teams was particularly enjoyable and it was encouraging to see how many of these young people went into various forms of full-time work for the Lord. Some went into the ministry. The down side was being away from the family so much. It was good when Liz went with him but on the whole there was a certain loneliness about it. The time came when we both felt that it was right for him to return to the pastoral ministry. He contacted the Baptist Union and began the process of finding a church.

We were invited to several churches, but didn't feel it was right until we were asked to go to Huddersfield, where there were two churches seeking ministry. The churches were quite close to each other and were linked but independent of each other. Bill would be Pastor of one and I the Pastor of the other. We met the people, took services and when they gave us a 'call' we felt, after prayer, that this was the right place for both of us. Bill would be Pastor of Primrose

Hill and I would be Pastor of Longley. We would live in the Primrose Hill Manse which was mid-way between the two churches.

There were certain things that had to be sorted out. I had to give the school three months notice. Bill was free to start right away. John was doing well at school and it was important that his next school should follow the same exam curriculum. Enquiries were made and part of our guidance to Huddersfield was the fact that two schools, Almondbury Grammar School and New College, followed the same syllabus and were prepared to have John join.

Leicestershire had gone over to the comprehensive system and had done away with the 11+ exam. John had passed the 11+ before we went to Fleckney. The Lord had wonderfully provided for this part of his future. John decided to go to New College, and it was to prove a tremendously beneficial provision for his education.

In order to get John grounded in his new school, he and Bill went to Huddersfield to live and Bill began his pastoral work at Primrose Hill. The official start of our ministries took place in the summer after Fiona and I joined Bill and John. During the three months, Fiona and I travelled up to Huddersfield for the weekend. We sang as we travelled and had happy times together; but we looked forward to the time when we would all be together again. It was the hot summer of 1976. When the Induction came in Huddersfield people stuck to their seats in the heat! Little did we know of the blessings that awaited us in Huddersfield.

12

"I've even stopped kicking the cat!"

The move to Huddersfield came at a very opportune time. I felt that I should now give up teaching and concentrate on ministry. The Longley Baptist Church was situated in an area of mixed housing. The council estates had gained some notoriety but were by no means as bad as others in Huddersfield. The church building was built as part of a Baptist Union drive to reach out to new developing areas. It had opened with a great flourish and the film record of the opening showed something of the excitement of this venture. Unfortunately it was 1939 and World War Two started soon afterwards. This meant that there were very real problems in establishing the church because of the lack of men and the other restrictions of war.

There were about 30 members when they called me to be their Pastor. They were not stuck in their ways but open to change. I quickly came to see that the leaders needed help in how to discern the way ahead for the church. It was all too easy for strong personalities to win any discussion. The first issue where this came to the fore was when we were discussing buying Bibles for the congregation to use. One deacon said, "We should go for the Good News. It's a good translation making it easy for people to understand." "I think we ought to stick with the more traditional version," said another. Neither was ready to give way to the other. The decision had to be postponed. As I prayed about the situation I felt God say to me, "Love is the key". He led me in bringing about reconciliation, and they came to a common mind. They opted for the Good News version. This was the beginning of establishing the vital place of Christian love in fellowship at Longley.

God gave me another clear 'word' that was to prove very significant for the church. I was travelling home from a fellowship meeting which was held in one of the homes, when I felt God say very clearly, "This is the meeting I shall use." It was a meeting held every fortnight and it met in various homes. The numbers grew, and because we needed a larger room it meant that we could only meet in a few of the houses. It continued to grow and we decided that we would have to meet in the church. Before long we had five groups meeting every week in various homes. The attendance at church on Sunday grew steadily and the newcomers were linked into one or other of the house groups. One year the Baptist Union stated that Longley was the fastest-growing Baptist church of its kind and published a paper about it with photographs.

What were the reasons for the growth? Certainly that word from the Lord, "Love is the key", was very important and I shall go into some detail of this later. One important factor was the first Church Away Weekend. This was held jointly with Bill's church at Primrose Hill and only three of our members, apart from myself, attended; but hey came back transformed by the Holy Spirit. People noticed and wanted to know the secret. Colin Urquhart had just published his book, *When the Spirit Comes*. This was found to be so helpful and challenging that copies were passed around the fellowship. People began asking, "Have you read Colin Urquhart's book?" The book was instrumental in enabling a number of people to experience the power of the Holy Spirit.

Isobel was one of those who started to attend the church. She was a very likeable person, but had had many unfortunate experiences in her life. There was a baptismal service being held at Primrose Hill and the Longley congregation joined with them. Bill made an appeal at the end of the service for people to come forward to receive Christ as Saviour and also for baptism. Isobel came forward. She said,

"God pushed me forward!" Her life was dramatically changed and she was the first to be baptised during my ministry at Longley.

One afternoon I had a phone call to say that Isobel's house was on fire and the fire service was in attendance. Bill and I went immediately. The firemen had left and we went into the building with Isobel. There was no real structural damage but the furnishings were completely ruined and nearly all that could burn was destroyed. Interestingly, certain combustible items survived. Among those items was a wooden cross made by her son at school, her Bible and a calendar with daily Bible texts. Very quickly the church people rallied round to her aid. The council provided a new house and the church folk furnished it. She ended up with a better house than she had before. But the significant thing was that the things that were burned were part of her old life. It became a very real sign to Isobel of the new life given to her by Jesus.

Norah was a very significant member of the congregation. She was in her seventies, renewed in the Holy Spirit and very much the evangelist. She particularly prayed that all her family would come to know Christ. The first to come to Him was her teenage grandson David. Although he was a helper in the Sunday School he was not a committed Christian. At the second Church Away Weekend with Primrose Hill there were considerably more from Longley than had attended the first. During one of the sessions David felt God calling him, but he argued against it. He said to God, "If You are calling me, let someone speak in tongues." He had never heard anyone speak in a Spirit-given language and was a bit sceptical. Andrew, one of the young men from Primrose Hill, spoke in a tongue during the meeting. Still unconvinced he said, "It could be coincidence. Let it happen again." It did. Still arguing with God he said, "God, if You are really calling me, send someone to me." Andrew was sitting fairly near David and he sensed that the Lord was speaking to him. "Can I help you?" he said to David. "Yes," said David, "and I want Glady to come too." Andrew beckoned me and we went out to another room. He told us of his struggle. Satan was really loath to let him go.

"I see the fires of hell!" he cried. This was a strange reaction because it was not the sort of thing I preached about – but it was certainly real to David. We prayed for him. He committed his life to Jesus and became very zealous in speaking to other young people about Him.

After one evening service a lady came to the church door begging for money to buy food and we gave her what we could. She started to come regularly to ask for money as folk were leaving the church. One day we met her son, John. He looked like a tramp. He had no teeth, his clothes were old and dirty and his hair long and unkempt. He said to me, "It's very kind of you to give money to my mother but I think you ought to know that she doesn't use it to buy food. She gambles it away."

"Thanks for letting us know, John. We'll give her food from now on." I said I would come and see her and try to help her with her finances.

Before this visit could be arranged, however, John visited me. "My mother has died. She stepped off a pavement without looking and a car knocked her down, and she died."

I sympathised with him and prayed for him. "Why not come to church, John. You'd be very welcome."

"What? Me? Welcome?"

"Of course. We'd love to see you."

Next Sunday evening John was waiting for me outside the church. He daren't go in alone among so many strangers. I welcomed him and explained, "I can't sit with you, John, because I have to lead the service. Come in and I'll introduce you to somebody who will sit with you." I had a word with Ian, one of the elders, and he called another leader over and both sat with John throughout the service.

From then on John never missed a service. He joined a house group and came to every meeting he could, even district meetings with other churches. Early on I organised a work party to do something about cleaning up his house. When we were there he kept walking down the path to the gate as if to say to his neighbours,

"These are my friends". His bedding was washed and his cat and dog were defleaed at the PDSA clinic.

John needed more than just help with the house. He was an alcoholic, so we paid for him to go to a Christian run rehabilitation centre to help him. He came back cured. One of the Elders helped him to smile – he was a dental technician and made him a set of teeth.

One day John said to me, "How can a man who died 2,000 years ago save me today?"

I felt that the best way of explaining this was to use the illustration of the bridge. I drew two cliffs separated by a chasm. "There's God on one side of the chasm," I said, "and we are on the other. We are separated from God by our sin. The Bible makes it clear that we can't jump across because the distance is too great and God is holy. No matter how 'good' we are we can never reach Him. We have all fallen short of His holiness. Paul says in Romans 3:23, 'all have sinned and fall short of the glory of God'. When Jesus died on the Cross it is as if the arms of the Cross form a bridge across this chasm." I drew the Cross forming this bridge over the chasm caused by sin. "The Bible tells us that Jesus bore our sin, for 'the Lord laid on him [i.e. Jesus] the iniquity of us all' (Isaiah 53:6 NIV). This has made it possible for us to come close to God. John, if you acknowledge your sin and thank Jesus for dying on your behalf, God will forgive you and so the way to Heaven will be opened up for you and you will go to be with Him forever." John understood, and as we prayed together he asked Jesus to be his Saviour. Later I was pleased to baptise him.

John moved from Longley some years later. He attended two other Baptist churches in the areas where he went to live. The Pastor called to see him one Saturday evening and they had a prayer together. He left John in his chair sitting by the fire. "See you in the morning, John," the Pastor said as he left. "You'll get your usual lift to church."

When the friends called to take him to church, John didn't answer

the door. Police were called and they found him as the Pastor had left him, in his chair with a half-drunk mug of tea and an open Bible. His death had obviously been sudden but peaceful.

We went to the funeral. It was standing room only! There were five ministers there! The undertaker was late in arriving at the church because he had difficulty finding it. The Pastor said, "This is the only time John has been late for church!"

There started to come into the fellowship a sense of expectancy that God was about to do something special. In one of the church prayer meetings we read from Haggai, "Today is the 24th day of the 9th month ... from now on I will bless you" (2:18-19). David, in his youthful enthusiasm and naivety, understood this to mean the 24th of September! It so happened that the 24th September was a Sunday, and David said to a group of us before the morning service, "Well, this is it!"

"This is what?" we asked.

"This is the day God's blessing is going to start!"

Remarkably, it was! God rewarded his simple faith and that evening two of the teenagers became Christians. Soon other people also committed themselves to Christ.

We decided as a church to go through the One Step Forward programme as a way of strengthening the fellowship. One part of the programme is 'Operation Agapë', which explores the principles of agapë – Christian Love. Everyone was given a workbook. The midweek meetings followed up the themes of the Sunday services based on an acrostic of 'AGAPE' and explored such subjects as 'Avoid criticism'; 'Go and visit'; 'Another acquaintance'; 'Pray for one another'; and 'Encourage one another'. This lasted for three months and the people really began to grasp the implications of Christian love. One day I visited a lady and we talked about the Operation Agapë programme. With marked enthusiasm she said to me, "It really works, this love thing! Do you know, I've even stopped kicking the cat"!

This exploration of Christian Love worked wonders for Longley; so much so that five years later we realised that half of the congregation had not done 'Operation Agapë'. So we went through it again. As God told me at the start of my ministry at Longley, love was indeed the key.

Another important element was the leadership of the church. One day God showed me who should be the leaders in certain areas. I called the existing leadership together and other obviously up and coming leaders and asked them to pray through the whole area of the leadership of the church at Longley. I did not tell them what I felt God had shown me. Some stepped down (graciously seeking the good of the church), others offered to do different jobs – and it was all as God had shown me!

I had finished the course for the Supplementary Minister's Course but the whole idea proved to be unsatisfactory. It was neither full ordination nor Lay Pastor. The Baptist Union recognised this and later dropped this form of ministry. As the fellowship grew I felt I should go for ordination, and in 1978 I was ordained. The call that God gave me was fulfilled even though it took 30 years! When God speaks, we have to learn to trust Him to bring about His purposes in His good time.

I felt led to teach series on church growth, prayer and healing. The church continued to grow and we began to see the implications of what it meant to be the Body of Christ, where each had a part to play using natural talents, acquired skills and spiritual gifts. The people were taking the Bible more seriously, "What does the Bible say? Am I acting upon it?" We began to see that we needed Elders. We took the matter slowly, ensuring that the church was in agreement with every step, and eventually we elected two Elders. They were father and son, Douglas and Ian. Later, as the church continued to grow, we added David and Pat. The fact that Pat was a woman was a new idea to many, but all the church were happy with her appointment; after all, they did have a woman minister! All

those who were appointed were already doing the work and it was more or less affirming them in their roles.

One of the very significant decisions was the formation of a ministry group. Some from Longley and Primrose Hill formed this group which we named Ichthus. Every member was born again and could clearly share a personal testimony. Each had been filled by the Holy Spirit and could minister to others. Some could take part in worship dance (which was a very recent innovation at that time), drama, and various forms of ministry. All could sing and were a very competent choir. They were invited to minister in different churches and led open-air services in Huddersfield town centre.

There was one very significant open-air meeting. When the group arrived to set up at the Piazza (a delightful area near the market and Town Hall) they were taken aback to see a very strong police presence and hundreds of angry protesters, most of whom were Asians. A very left-wing speaker was speaking very belligerently. We learned that the National Front had announced a march that day either in Leeds or Huddersfield. The National Front had deliberately been vague in order to get maximum effect. The police had to take preventative action in both towns. Bill went to a high-ranking officer and explained about the Open Air. "What should we do?" he asked, expecting the officer to say they had enough to do without being bothered with a church open-air meeting.

Surprisingly he said, "Stay here and be ready. We should learn soon about whether or not the march will take place in Huddersfield."

The announcement came. The officer addressed the crowd. "The National Front is marching in Leeds. You can all go home." He turned to Bill: "Right. Go ahead."

Quickly, Ichthus danced, sang, shared testimony, etc. The crowd mostly stayed and entered into what was being done. Everything was in good humour and the Lord used the group to help diffuse what could have been a very nasty situation and, of course, to share the Gospel.

A wonderful sense of unity developed among the churches of the area. The ministers of some of the local churches (Anglican, Baptist and Methodist) began meeting together on a regular basis and from this there developed 'The Castle Group of Churches'. We decided on this name because all the churches were situated around Castle Hill in Huddersfield. All the ministers and their churches were evangelical and charismatic and wanted to explore the ways and gifts of the Holy Spirit. We had a monthly rally in one of the churches each month. We had church holidays together and would go to a large Victorian mansion near Knaresborough called Allerton Park for weekends and even for a week. God did many wonderful things through this group of churches.

As a result of all that God was doing some from Longley and Primrose Hill felt very strongly that God was calling them together to live in community. A large old Jacobean house came on the market and those interested in community living went to view it. The house was not suitable, but visiting it brought about heart searching within the group as to just what would be involved in such a commitment. Some felt it was right to pursue the idea. Others, for various reasons, felt they could not make the commitment of actually living in the same house, but still wanted to support the venture.

Bill and I were living in the Primrose Hill Church Manse as part of our calling to the ministries at the two churches. To live in such a community would cause problems, so we could not be part of the venture, but wholly supported it. A large semi became available in an ideal spot between the two churches. Two families, both from Primrose Hill, sold their homes and jointly moved in. Amazingly, the other identical semi became available fairly soon after and a family from Longley moved in. With some alterations the whole property had 13 bedrooms. The house was given the name, 'Bethnimrah' – The House of Sweet(or Healing) Waters. It was to live up to its name.

Wonderful things happened at Primrose Hill. New people came and a significant number of students attended regularly. Then, after

117

some years, some started to want the "old ways" and hindered the coming of change. The students no longer felt welcome and others started to drift away. Bill had to face up to what the Lord was saying. He was due a sabbatical and he spent it praying through what God was saying. God clearly confirmed his call to the ministry and the nature of his ministry. He felt he had no option but to resign his ministry at Primrose Hill. He shared this first with the leadership and then the church. In time the Lord made it clear that Bill should join me at Longley. Some others felt the same and, independently of Bill, decided to attend Longley. One of the things that had to be worked out was where were we to live? The result of all this was that Bill and I went to live at Bethnimrah. John had gone to University. Fiona was a keen young Christian and she was happy about the move.

Bill and I had developed our own ministries but saw eye to eye on everything. The church at Longley knew Bill well because we frequently exchanged pulpits and linked together in different ways. Bill was appointed as joint minister with me. His coming strengthened the leadership, for he had skills I did not have and we complemented each other in a wonderful way.

There was a strong sense in the church that evangelism was a vital element. The church used and developed several forms of evangelising the neighbourhood. 'Door knocking' was one and there were a good number who were ready to listen to what we had to share. Quite a few people started coming to church through this means. We held open-air meetings on the village green and these were always well received. We also used a programme called, "Good News Down the Street" to teach people in their homes the basics of the Gospel.

From time to time there were evangelistic efforts organised by the Huddersfield Churches to reach the people of the town. Longley provided several trained counsellors and stewards. In 1984 Billy Graham held a series of meetings in Sheffield at the Bramhall Lane football ground, the home of Sheffield United. Longley was very much involved in taking people there. Bill and I were Advisers in the counselling area. Another great town event was "Praise for Pentecost" which grew from an original idea by Bill. Huddersfield Town Hall was filled to capacity for this great gathering every Pentecost Sunday.

Bethnimrah became an important part of the church's life. Monthly there was a "bring and share" meal and various other events like the church Bonfire took place there. From time to time various people came for short or long term counselling. The adult members of the Community met every week for fellowship and guidance. We all had jobs to do and shared equally in the financial commitments.

All who lived at Bethnimrah had a strong commitment to each other, to the church and, above all, to Jesus. Friday night was kept as a time when the family units stayed in their own family lounges. This was particularly important for the young children who needed to know who Mummy and Daddy were. Being in family units on a Friday evening was keeping in line with the principle that the church developed, that "Friday night is family night". As the church grew, and got more and more involved in all sorts of ventures, we recognised the need to reserve one evening when we would not organise any Church activity. It was an important aspect of the church's life.

The community at Bethnimrah ran for some years. One of the folk we ministered to was Colin. He was an alcoholic and could be violent when drunk. On one occasion when he was drunk he threw a large stone through one of the large front windows of Bethnimrah. He had had a dreadful childhood which was the root cause for his behaviour. When sober he would produce very good art work and write poems. Bill helped him sort out his finances and I saw him regularly for counselling. Normally, Bill would counsel men and I women, but the basic root of Colin's problems was a brutish father and he responded better to me than to Bill.

One evening, after midnight, there was loud knocking on the door of Bethnimrah. Bill got out of bed and opened the door to find Colin

in a drunken rage. "I want to see Glady."

"Glad's in bed. She's expecting you to come and see her in the morning. Go home to bed, Colin."

"I want to see Glad and I want to see her NOW!"

"Be reasonable, Colin. She's tired."

"I want to see her NOW!" he roared and at that, grabbed Bill round the throat. Bill instantly felt the Presence of the Lord and committed the situation to Him. He did not struggle. Colin just grunted and stopped and left. Bill came to bed and shared what had gone on.

Next morning, as arranged, Colin came for counselling and also to sort out some finance problem with Bill. He was full of apologies for his behaviour. They prayed together. Years later when we came back to Yorkshire to minister, Colin came to see us to welcome us back to Yorkshire. He had travelled some distance in very heavy rain to see us. It was good to learn that he was making something of his life.

There were many occasions when I had to deal with very difficult problems. One lunch time, as I was serving the meal at home, I was called out to a woman who was trying to take her own life. Then, one Christmas afternoon I spent the time in a police cell. A young man, who sometimes came to our church, had been arrested for stabbing his father. He asked if I could see him. He was later found guilty of killing his brutish father. I regularly visited him in Wakefield Jail where he was serving a life sentence.

There came a time when Andrew, who with his wife Barbara, was a part owner of the property, felt he should change his job. He was being asked to do things which he felt he could not do because of his Christian faith. This became an important matter for prayer in the Community. He was asked to go to Peterborough for an interview. He was not at all sure as to whether to go or not. As we all in Bethnimrah prayed together there came a clear instruction for Andrew: "Go and the Lord will make His will clear." Andrew went and as he sat in the secretary's office waiting to be called for the

interview the secretary said to him, "Are you a Christian?" She had noticed his fish badge. "Yes," said Andrew. "We've been praying for a Christian to apply for this job."

Andrew was amazed and wondered what would be the outcome of the interview. When he went in to see the manager there was the same conversation, "We've been praying that a Christian will apply for this job." Andrew put every obstacle he could think of before the manager and each one was met. He was offered the job and the Community prayed it through with him. Against everyone's personal inclinations, the Lord's will was made clear: "Take the job."

Andrew and Barbara and their young family went to Peterborough. This meant they had to sell their part of the property and we all discerned that Bethnimrah should end. It had fulfilled its purpose. We were all sorry to let it go. "The Lord gave. The Lord has taken away. Blessed be the name of the Lord". It had been a rich time for all those involved.

The remaining members of the community had to buy houses, and in wonderful ways the Lord led them all so that they remained very much part of Longley. The Longley Church had no Manse and so we had to find a property. We found a delightful semi-detached property near the church. Later, two of the Elders moved nearby and the street was nicknamed "Elders' Row"!

In the autumn of 1985 the Area Superintendent of Yorkshire passed on to us a request from a Baptist Minister in Australia called Jack Measham. He was interested in a three month exchange with a Baptist Minister in England.

"When this request came to me," said the Area Superintendent, "I thought of you two. It would be for February to April next year. Are you interested?"

The idea appealed to us and we prayed about it. Fiona had been accepted for University and so would be in Halls of Residence. We felt it would be good for the church to have experience of another minister. After prayer and discussion it was felt right to pursue the

proposal for the exchange. The idea was acceptable to Longley and the Church at Geelong in Victoria, Australia, and we exchanged with Jack.

It proved to be a great experience for all concerned. We exchanged what was to be a very cold and snowy winter for a glorious late summer. We loved the sun and Jack and his family delighted in experiencing real snow. It proved a time of refreshing for us. We needed to ease off a bit from the pressures of the developing church at Longley, whilst it benefited from the different style of leadership that Jack gave. We found real friendship in the church at Geelong and over the years a number of the fellowship came and stayed with us in England.

There was an interesting incident when the time came for us to fly home. Our flight out of Melbourne was scheduled to stop at Bali and it so happened that President Ronald Reagan was in Bali. This caused chaos for those flights into and out of Bali.

We had to go to a specially designated area where everyone and everything was thoroughly checked. There was zero tolerance regarding excess baggage and people were opening cases and passing things on to those who had come to see them off. Some had to arrange for such excess luggage to be sent on separately at a later date. We knew we had excess luggage because we had been showered with presents at our farewell gathering and we had bought presents to take home. We had bought a large case to carry them and our basic luggage took up our weight allowance.

As we waited to get our bags weighed a couple pushed in front of us in the queue. There was no need for such behaviour and our first reaction was to make some kind of gentle protest. We didn't because there was no real point. It would not prevent us from getting on the plane. A young man was getting his bags weighed and he went aside to take articles out to lighten the load. The couple who had barged in, put their bags to be weighed – it totalled just two flight bags!

They moved on with no problems. We put ours on the scales and waited for the attendant to instruct us to do something about our excess luggage. He just carried on, put labels on all our bags and said to us, "You're overweight but I've linked you with the two who've just gone through. You can make your way to the flight"! We never saw those two again. We wondered if God had sent a couple of angels to help us through! It seemed so unlikely that a couple would be travelling with so little luggage.

When we returned to the Longley church there was a huge banner on the platform:

WELCOME HOME, GLAD AND BILL

Australia was a wonderful experience that we still treasure, but we were glad to be back with our dear friends at Longley.

One evening I was baby-sitting for Tony and Kath so that they could go to a house group together. The phone rang.

"Is Tony there?"

"I'm sorry, he's out. Can I take a message?"

"I'm in great need and I just don't know who to turn to. I live in Barnsley and I knew Tony when he was seeking election to the Council. His poster mentioned that he was a Christian. I don't know any other person who is a Christian and I feel I need a Christian to help me. My teenage son has become very violent. He struck me with a spade. I'm terrified of what he'll do. I'm a spiritualist. I feel I need the help of somebody who knows God better than I do. Do you think he could help?"

"I'll pass on the message. What's your number?"

I noted her number and told Tony when he came in.

"Much as I would like to help this woman," said Tony, "I feel this is beyond my experience. I think it's a job for you and Bill if you think you can give the time."

We had previously ministered to Tony and Kath in connection with demonic activity associated with their house, so they were aware

of what was involved in this kind of ministry. I shared it with Bill when I got home and we prayed it through. We both felt that this was a cry for help that the Lord wanted us to respond to. I telephoned the lady and we made a time to see her and her husband.

They were waiting for us when we arrived. "It's good of you to come all this way to see us and we appreciate your willingness to help us. We feel at our wits' end about what has happened."

"Tell us about your problem," I said.

There was an obvious sense of relief as they felt we were genuinely seeking to help them. The wife told the story. "We have an 18-year-old son. For some time now his lifestyle has deteriorated. He refuses to wash. He only wants to watch horror and sex movies. He flatly refuses to help in any way in the house."

The husband took over the story as she found it difficult to continue. "Things came to a head when he started to become violent. A couple of days ago he attacked his mother with a spade. We felt something had to be done but we didn't want to involve the police or social services. We love our son. He needs help. And then Tony's name came into our minds. We liked what we learned about him at the time of the election and so rang him. Can you help us?"

"When did the problems start with your son?" I asked.

"It was when we became spiritualists. He was twelve at the time."

"Tell us about your experience of spiritualism."

"I had a spirit guide who enabled me to be used in healing," said the wife.

"Did you see people healed?"

"Oh yes, but what I found strange was that while others seemed to get healed I got all sorts of illnesses!"

Bill asked the husband, "And what did you experience?"

"I had the gift of automatic writing! A spirit guide gave me all sorts of messages."

We explained that spiritualism was contrary to what God wants for His people. We quickly showed Biblical passages to back up our statement.

"If it's wrong, we want to give it up," was their joint reply.

We explained the way of salvation to them and they both accepted Jesus as their Saviour. We prayed with them and released them from the bondage caused by their dabbling with spiritualism.

"Where's your son?" asked Bill.

"He's upstairs in his bedroom."

"Can we see him?"

"Of course, I'll fetch him," said the father.

The mother said to us, "You will be gentle with him, won't you?"

"Of course."

The youth appeared with his father and sat down. We listened to his story. "I don't know why I hit Mum. Something came over me." Gently we explained things to him and then, with a simple prayer, we cast out the evil spirit in him and asked the Holy Spirit to fill him. Afterwards he came over and shook our hands and said, "Thank you very much for helping me." The parents sat open-mouthed at his politeness! Next day the mother phoned. "After you left our lad asked, 'Can I help you with the dishes?' He then asked for a bath!" We linked the family with a local church where they could get the pastoral care they needed.

As at Leigh Park we saw God at work in many wonderful ways. There were a number of healings of all types. One such healing came one Christmas. A couple had a boy born just before Christmas. He was a big baby but had severe breathing problems and was kept in hospital after the mother was allowed home. He was kept in an oxygen tent. The parents rang us on the morning of Christmas Eve. "Will you and Bill go to the hospital and anoint Matthew with oil, please?"

"Of course we will. We'll go this afternoon."

They arranged to meet us at the hospital. In the church we often anointed people with oil following the teaching in James 5. We met the parents at the church and made our way to where the baby was being given intensive care. The medical people were happy for Bill

and me to go into the tent. We prayed for his healing and anointed him. There was an immediate change in his condition! We left the parents there. They later rang us. "Matthew's so improved that we can bring him home!" It was a delightful Christmas present for the family. Matthew, like the other brothers who would be born, grew up with the typical build of a rugby prop forward!

At one of the church prayer gatherings in several ways there came a very clear word from the Lord: "Plan for growth". We took God at His word and ordered more hymn books, more Bibles, more chairs and affirmed another Elder. It was also decided that we should extend the church building. God kept His word. Every Sunday that year (except one) new people came to the church and there was a record number of baptisms. Many of the people were on low incomes, but all in the church responded with joyful generosity towards the new extension. Much of the work was done by the fellowship. Ian, a qualified architect, designed the extension and supervised the work. Bill did much of the interior work and many in the fellowship did all manner of tasks.

The opening of the extension was one of the highlights of our time in Longley. The church's 50th anniversary coincided with the opening of the new extension. As part of the celebrations over the weekend we held a flower festival. This was a new venture for the church and revealed an amazing array of talent within the fellowship. I had been invited as a guest speaker at a church in Scarborough during a time when they held a flower festival for summer visitors. They had based the displays on the theme of 'Faith', with Hebrews 11 as the basic scripture. Many visitors were attracted to the Festival and I saw the value of such an event. The displays for our weekend were based on events in John's Gospel. As people arrived at the porch they saw a display representing Jesus, 'The Light of the World'. As they entered the church John the Baptist was portrayed, a sandal and leather belt on the sand and a dove hovering over Jordan. And so it went on as people moved round the church. The events of Holy Week were represented on the lower platform with the climax on the

upper platform depicting the Crucifixion and the Resurrection. It was a stunning display by the contributors and showed their spiritual grasp of the events in John's Gospel.

The main service of thanksgiving for fifty years and the dedication of the new extension were celebrated on the Saturday afternoon. The church was packed. As well as our own folk there were past members and ministers and representatives of various churches and organisations. When the offering was being taken, and a worship song was being played, one of the girls from the Junior Worship Dance Group got up and spontaneously danced to the Lord. Everyone was blessed by this. The Deputy Lord Mayor was due to speak immediately after. As he rose he was moved to tears and found words difficult. "God is in this place!" he said and he was voicing the feeling of all who were present.

The time came for the oldest member to cut the ribbon and open up the way to the new extension, and the youngest member cut the special cake. Afterwards we all went upstairs to have a meal in the new hall. It was a truly memorable weekend. Soon afterwards Fiona obtained her degree in optometry and married Andy who was one of the members at Longley. They were the first to hold a wedding reception in the new hall. They moved up to the Newcastle area where Fiona had her first appointment as an optometrist.

Over the years I had become increasingly aware of an ache in my right hip. I was born with shallow hips and this led to a deterioration of the cartilage in the joint. I knew that the time would come when I would need a hip replacement. That time arrived in 1986. I saw a surgeon in Bradford. "There's no doubt you need a hip replacement. The cartilage in your right hip has completely worn away. It will be three months before I can operate. There's not much we can do regarding the pain in the meantime, but at least you know that come Easter the pain will be gone." The pain was excruciating and yet through it all I had a wonderful sense of God holding me above the pain. As Easter 1987 approached, I was called to the Bradford

127

Orthopaedic Hospital at Woodlands on the border of Bradford and Leeds.

Mr Nevelos, the surgeon, said to me, "You lead too active a life to be fitted with the usual Charnley hip. Were you retired, and just pottering about the house, the Charnley hip would be fine. But because you're so active I'm going to give you the latest type of ceramic hip. It should last for much longer. It will mean, however, a longer stay in hospital and a longer time using weight-bearing crutches, but it will be worth it." I felt it was worth all the inconvenience for the better type of hip replacement.

When a friend of mine heard I would have at least two weeks in hospital she offered to pay for a private room for me. "Thank you very much," I said, "it's very kind of you, but I feel that one of the reasons why I will be in hospital is so that I can be a witness for Jesus." She fully understood. It was a great encouragement to me to know that I had such wonderful friends. So, instead of a private room I was in an open ward with 24 beds.

What a varied group! There was Pat, a Mormon staying away from her church because she had started drinking and smoking and they didn't approve of such behaviour. Betty, a Catholic who had lost her husband in the war and had to bring up two children on her own. Angie, crude and earthy but seeking the Lord. There was Sybil who was 73, had pink dyed hair, bright red nails and lips and was for ever 'price dropping'. There was a regular churchgoer called Dorothy who was visited by ladies from her church. Liz, who had eight children and had been in and out of hospital for the past three years, queried whether there could be a god. Dolores worried about her husband who was in the Bradford Royal Infirmary with a serious heart condition. My companions for two weeks!

They laughed and joked, spoke crudely about sex. I joined in as best I could without compromising my Christian faith. They respected my Christian stance. I had many private conversations and a number opened up to me, sharing their problems and their questions.

One morning as I was reading my Bible, Angie, in the bed opposite mine, asked out loud, "What are you reading, Glad?"

"The Bible."

"Well, read it to us."

So I read them the story of Jesus healing Peter's mother-in-law.

"Now it's your turn," said Angie, nodding to the lady in the bed next to me. "There's a Bible in your locker. Choose something."

She went round the whole ward in the same manner! Everyone read something. "Let not your hearts be troubled" was read by Sybil. Pat read the Beatitudes. Lots of questions were raised and it was a wonderful opportunity of witness. Angie asked me over to go through Acts 2. Liz, in the bed next to Angie, said, "I'm afraid of dying." I referred to the words Sybil had read, "Let not your heart be troubled." I was able to explain the way of salvation to both Liz and Angie by referring to the words of Jesus in Revelation 3:20, "Behold, I stand at the door and knock. If anyone hears my voice and opens the door I will come in."

I had many visitors during my time in hospital. The family travelled the length and breadth of the country and many came from the church. My darling Bill came every day and travelled a total of 700 miles!

After being at Longley for over 12 years we began to sense that we should consider moving to another church. We felt that it would be good for the church to have a change of minister. The three months when Jack from Australia led the church had shown them a different style of leadership and they had benefited from it. When our proposal was shared with the church many wept and some were inconsolable, but they came to recognise the leading of the Lord.

Liz and Sean had come to live in Huddersfield by this time and were members at Longley. The thought of leaving them and the three grandchildren was a real wrench. However, our leaving proved to be a significant event for them, for it was the means of developing Liz as a leader in the Church. She became a Deacon and a Pastoral

Visitor and regularly preached. This led to her call to the Baptist Ministry. We were called to a church that was very different from Longley – the Church of the Redeemer in Edgbaston, Birmingham.

13

"Go and look at bungalows"

The Church of the Redeemer in Birmingham was an influential church. For a hundred years the great Victorian edifice, more like a cathedral than a Baptist Church, stood on the Hagley Road. Changes in the area and structural problems with the building caused a lot of heart searching regarding the future of the church. In the 1970s it was decided to sell the building and move round the corner into Monument Road. A large cinema site was bought and a beautiful modern church building erected. Linked in with the church building was a complex of over forty flats for the elderly and a day-care centre. The first minister in the new building had dynamic leadership qualities and the church grew rapidly. There were special concerns for the poor and the marginalised of society. A hostel for homeless young people was purchased and a warden appointed. An Advice Bureau was set up and a youth and community worker appointed. With great energy and innovation the church sought to make a difference in the community, particularly in nearby Ladywood where there was much deprivation. The whole city became aware of the impact of the Church.

Sadly, problems arose regarding the leadership which resulted in the minister being asked to leave. Others also left and the church floundered. Many went to other churches. We were asked to come and bring healing to a church divided and hurting. We prayed about the situation. There was so much that drew us to the

church and at the same time there was the awareness of the enormous task. God made it clear that we should accept the church's invitation to be the joint ministers and we accepted – but with some trepidation.

A number of people who attended the church did so because of the church's stance on issues like racism, feminism, the priority of children, and so on. We shared these concerns and preached about them, but we did not make the same emphases as the previous minister. We felt that the basic message of the Gospel had been neglected in favour of its more marginal aspects. This didn't please some and so they decided to leave. A number came to us for counselling because of past hurts to do with what had happened in the church. We were able to bring inner healing to quite a number. Often after such ministry the response of those we helped was, "Thank you for helping me. Now that I'm freed from past hurts I can move on in my Christian life. I think it would be better for me if I left Redeemer and attend a church nearer where I live." We understood that, and encouraged them to attend a more local church instead of travelling across the city to Redeemer, but it meant a reduction in numbers.

An exodus began. Some were malcontents who were not happy with our ministry. Some, as I've said, decided to attend more local churches. It was a difficult time for us and we almost dreaded hearing the phone ring to tell us of another who wanted to leave. New people started to come and the church started to build up again. However, there was still something wrong at its heart.

There was something lacking and those who were spiritually sensitive were very aware of it. Jennie, from Longley, visited us and told us, "I was so looking forward to the worship but somehow I felt I couldn't express praise and adoration." Others in the fellowship spoke of "heaviness", "fog", and a "quenching of the Spirit". There came a time when our own doctor, who was a Deacon and completely behind our leadership, came to us one day and said, "I will have to leave or I shall lose my faith. I advise you to do the same." But God had a work for us to do and we felt we must bring healing to this sick church.

In the midst of all the problems there were wonderful joys and much for which we praised God. We hadn't been at the church long when we went one evening to visit a young couple who had recently married. They were both doctors working in the same hospital. After the meal they had prepared for us Simon said to us, "We'd like you to have this." And he gave us a couple of car keys. "Now that we're married we don't need two cars. You two have to visit folk all over Birmingham, so you could do with a second car." We were touched and amazed at their generosity! Their minds were made up and they were sure of the Lord's guidance. With gladness Simon gave us his old but serviceable car that had served him well through his years of training. Bill drove the car home and we now had greater flexibility in dealing with the pastoral demands of the church. The car was to serve us well for the next few years and was a confirmation to us that we were right to come to Redeemer.

There were those in the church who were gifted in writing sketches, which meant that we were able to worship with a rich contribution from people in the church. A banner group provided added colour to the building with some beautiful creations. There was a monthly youth service that especially involved the Scouts and Guides of the church. I helped with the Girl Guides and they gave me the name "Blue Tit".

The Hostel for Homeless Young People did useful work. We called in there on various occasions. One of the things we did was to invite the residents of the hostel to come to our house for tea on a Saturday each month. The Manse which the church bought for us was a large house with a large lounge where we could entertain friends. It gave the youngsters a taste of being in a home. We had a dog Gypsy and they enjoyed playing with him. They loved to play all sorts of family games with us. We never probed into their backgrounds, but some did share something of their stories. Through the hostel many were enabled to make a decent start in life.

133

We bought Gypsy at a dogs' home in Birmingham. He was a border collie cross. He was well trained and loved people. The front window of our lounge had a low window sill and he liked to stand with his front paws on the window ledge and look at people as they passed. For some reason he always barked when someone passed wearing a hat! It was never an angry bark. One afternoon after I left to do some pastoral visiting and Bill was just about to go out, he heard Gypsy barking; but it was an angry bark.

He went to see what was causing Gypsy to react in this way and saw that he was barking at a young man on the opposite side of the street. He was punching a young girl who was trying to get into the phone box to protect herself. Gypsy recognised this as wrong behaviour.

Bill went across the road to help the girl and the young man ran off. The girl had taken some blows to the face. "Would you like to come over to my house? I'll make you a cup of coffee," said Bill and explained that he was a Baptist minister. He also made it clear he was alone in the house. She nodded and came over. Bill went to make coffee and when he came into the lounge the girl was stroking Gypsy and was obviously a great deal calmer than when she came in the house. Gypsy sensed her need.

She told Bill her story: that her boyfriend wanted her to get involved in prostitution. He hit her when she refused and she had run away from the flat they shared. He had caught up with her at the telephone kiosk. Bill prayed with her and took her round to the hostel. There were no vacancies, but the Warden was able to get her a place in another hostel. A few weeks later she called round to thank Bill for his help. Gypsy was there at the door and she fussed him. "By the way," she said to Bill, "I don't like dogs. I'm scared of them; but Gypsy is an exception!" He was a hero!

We had very good relationships with the local churches and met together at a monthly Sunday evening gathering. Close to Redeemer was The Oratory, the Roman Catholic Church founded by Cardinal Newman. The ministers met there regularly to plan the various

events. Bill and I spoke regularly at the morning assembly of the nearby St George's Junior School. Another interesting aspect of our ministry was that Bill and I were asked by the local group of Christian Doctors to counsel some of their patients who would benefit more from counselling than from medication.

Myrtle was one of the key members of Redeemer. She was among the original group of Afro-Caribbeans who came over to this country in the 1950s. One of the things she was looking forward to at that time was being part of the Church life in England. She had attended a church at the first opportunity. She found the service a bit staid, but she could cope with that. As she was leaving the church the minister said to her, "We hope you enjoyed the service but I would be grateful if you don't come again. Our people are very set in their ways and they're not used to a black person in the congregation." Myrtle was shocked and deeply felt the rejection; but she would not be put off going to church. Next Sunday she attended another church and the response was similar. This went on for several weeks. Different churches and different denominations, but always the same response – "Please don't come again."

When she came to the Church of the Redeemer, however, she was welcomed with open arms. They were delighted to have her presence and the insights she brought. She became a key person bringing a special brand of spirituality to the congregation. She was one of the first people we got to know at Redeemer and a special relationship developed between us.

A number of the residents from the flats built as part of the church complex came to the church. We regularly visited and saw a number deepen their faith. One of the residents who was a church member was George Rice. He had been in the First World War and was blinded. It was lovely sharing fellowship with him and his wife. He had a radiant faith. He was one of the oldest survivors of the Great War and lived to be well over 100.

Mary was a delightful old lady who moved into one of the flats when she was finding it difficult to cope with the stairs in her house.

135

At one service I gave the people an acorn and invited them to see if God would speak to them using the acorn as a visual aid. I asked the people to share anything that God had said to them. Mary was one of the first to respond and it was all the more remarkable because she was very timid and reserved. "God said to me, 'Come out of your shell'." And she did! She subsequently prayed openly and would take part in discussions. It was wonderful to see this elderly lady opening out.

The extraordinary readiness to accept people regardless of their background was one of the great strengths of Redeemer. A couple in the church had been visiting a man serving a prison sentence. Largely through their influence he became a Christian while in prison and took a course on discipleship. When he was released he came to live near the church and started attending. He soon felt at home with the worship and the people. He was welcomed into membership and in time became a Deacon.

Near the church there was a home for people with learning difficulties. They had a variety of problems. One man every now and again would go missing. Somehow he managed to get into trains and would end up in various places in the country. Practically the whole group of residents attended morning service and were wonderfully accepted by the congregation. In their simple way they shared in the life of the church.

The Chinese Church in Birmingham asked if they could use the premises of Redeemer on Sunday afternoons. The church happily agreed to this and Bill and I preached regularly. For a time they didn't have a Pastor and Bill was asked to baptise quite a number of them. It was something of a problem to pronounce their Chinese names when baptising them! The Service was in Chinese and so when we preached it was through an interpreter. This was a new experience for us. When one of us was due to preach, the person appointed to interpret would come some days before to vet the sermon for expressions and idioms that would be difficult to translate. Humour could also be a problem, particularly with the

elderly people who spoke little or no English. It was interesting to see that when we shared a joke the students would laugh after we related the joke and the elderly people would laugh after the translation!

We were very privileged to be asked by a couple in the Chinese Church to act as the bride's parents at their planned wedding ceremony. Her parents lived in Hong Kong and were unable to come to England. We were delighted to accept. She was married wearing a traditional British white wedding gown and, as her 'mother', I helped her dress. Bill escorted her down the aisle. The Chinese Pastor conducted the ceremony. After the ceremony I helped her change into a traditional crimson Chinese gown. The Chinese fashion is for the newly-married couple to arrive last at the reception with the bride's parents. We arrived to a great welcome and thoroughly enjoyed the Chinese celebration of marriage.

Since Redeemer had a Manse it meant that we had some money that we wanted to invest in getting another property. We felt that this would help as an investment towards buying a house when we retired. We started to look around for a house that could be used for holidays and also be available to others. We looked at a map and noted that the quickest way to the country from Edgbaston was along the A456 towards Kidderminster and then the River Severn area. On our day off one week we went to Kidderminster to see what it was like and what was available in our price range. All that was available was in Kidderminster itself and was not rural enough for what we were looking for. "You'll have to pay another £10,000 for the same thing in the country," the estate agents told us.

On another day off we tried the Redditch area. It was not rural enough either. "To get a place in the country with what you want will cost you another £10,000 on your price." It was not looking hopeful. We returned from Redditch with a load of leaflets and information about houses for sale. Later that night, as I was looking through the various leaflets we had been given, one brochure caught my eye.

"Where's Highley?" I wondered.

"I've no idea. I've never heard of it. Why do you ask?"

"There's an advert here about a house in Highley that seems to have what we're looking for and in our price range!"

We looked on the map and found it to be a village by the River Severn in South Shropshire. It was close to the Wyre Forest. Everything seemed to suggest this was the rural situation we were hoping to find – a village, river and forest!

We rang the estate agent on Monday. "Is it still available?" "Yes," came the reply and we decided to drop everything and go. We went to the agents in Bewdley for the key to view the property. As we travelled north from Bewdley we drove through the pretty little villages of Button Oak and Button Bridge in the beautiful Wyre Forest. We fell in love with the forest.

Highley, we discovered, was large enough to have several shops. The house we came to view was part of a Victorian terrace with access to open fields where we could walk Gypsy. We bought the house. Bill renewed the kitchen units. George, the next-door neighbour, was a keen gardener and he was happy to keep our plot tidy and grow vegetables for himself on it. The house had a happy, friendly feel about it and we enjoyed the times we were able to spend there. A number of ministers were able to come and enjoy a free relaxing holiday. It was wonderful to have this asset just 45 minutes away from Birmingham.

My Aunt Louie was living on her own in Edinburgh. She was 90 and beginning to be rather frail but wouldn't admit it. I felt that the time had come when she should seriously think of coming to live with us. Bill agreed. I put it to her and eventually she agreed to come, but wanted one more Christmas in her home in Edinburgh. On Christmas Eve her neighbour, who was a doctor, called to give her a Christmas card and present. She didn't answer his knock and he sensed something was wrong. He looked through the window and saw her slumped in her chair. He rang 999 and Louie was taken into the Edinburgh Royal Infirmary nearby. She had been immobilised through a deep vein thrombosis in her leg. In hospital they

recognised she had a very serious condition and also found that she had cancer. They contacted me and we went up to Edinburgh. I was told that her condition was very serious.

"How serious is her condition?" I asked.

"Perhaps three months."

"Can she come to stay with me in Birmingham?"

A conference was held and it was agreed that she should stay in hospital a little longer to stabilise her and then she could come down to Birmingham. Although Louie was so ill she was very peaceful. Her strong Christian faith meant that death was not a problem for her.

We had to deal with her belongings and organise the sale of her house. Fortunately a buyer was quickly found for the house and with the help of my cousin Charlie and his wife Lilly the contents were dealt with. Louie came down by ambulance from Edinburgh to Birmingham and she enjoyed the ride! Sadly, she didn't spend Christmas in her home, but she looked forward to staying with us. The Manse was a large house with a ground floor bedroom and bathroom and was ideally suited for her. Despite the expectations of the doctors in Edinburgh Louie was to have another six full years of life.

After about three months of care Louie was able to get about in her wheelchair. When she was able we took her to our little house in Highley. She loved everything about it, but because she couldn't negotiate stairs for the bedroom and the bathroom it was totally unsuitable for her. The three of us discussed the situation together and decided to look for a bungalow. We found the ideal bungalow on the edge of Highley. One day, without explaining to Louie, we said, "We're going to take you out for a ride." "Where are we going?" "It's a surprise." Louie loved surprises and so eagerly anticipated the outing. We arrived at the bungalow. It could be perfect for Louie, its large entrance hall enabling her to negotiate the various rooms. The garden was such that she could sit for hours and enjoy the sun. The house had been empty for two years and the garden was very

overgrown, but that could be sorted out. There was one snag – the price! It was just under £90,000. Even with Louie's help that was beyond us. We would have to look elsewhere.

One Thursday, as I was ironing, I felt the Lord say to me, "Go and look at bungalows."

I argued: "I can't do that today, Lord. Friday is our day off. We'll go tomorrow."

The voice persisted, "Go and look at bungalows."

I told Bill about what God had been saying to me.

"You go," said Bill. "There must be some reason for God's insisting you go today."

I went to the Estate Agents in Bewdley who were handling the bungalow we had seen in Highley. "I want to see some bungalows." "Certainly," said the young lady. "I'll take you to see some we have in the neighbourhood." She took me to see several in our price range, but all had an entrance corridor rather than a hall and so would have been very difficult for Louie. We went back to the Estate Agents' office and talked further about our particular requirements for Louie.

"The ideal bungalow is the one we saw at Highley. That would suit us very well. The problem is the price. It's very much beyond what we can afford."

The estate agent pricked up her ears when I mentioned Highley. "Which bungalow was that?"

"The one in Cherry Bank. The asking price of nearly £90,000 is way beyond what we can afford."

"Cherry Bank, you say? Wait here a minute. I want to have a word with my colleague." She returned very shortly. "That bungalow was repossessed by the mortgage company this morning. You'll be able to get it cheaper."

"How much cheaper?"

"Try £65,000"!

I returned home excited. We discussed the matter.

"I don't understand how it is that previous mortgage lenders have repossessed the house," I said. "It has been empty for two years and

no one has lived there since the previous owner moved out. I wouldn't consider this option if it meant pushing somebody out of their home. It seems that somehow or other the Lord has kept this bungalow until we were in a position to buy it!"

"Let's go for it!" said Lou, and we all agreed.

We rang the Estate Agents. "We'll put in an offer of £65,000," I said.

"Good," was the reply. "It's an offer you just can't refuse. The procedure is that the mortgage lender must advertise the property for a further week to see if there are any higher bids for the property. I'll be in touch."

A week later the phone rang. "No one has put in a higher bid for the property. We can go ahead with the sale."

We soon got a buyer for the house we had in Highley and the sale went through with little difficulty. Once again the Lord had led us – but just what was the story behind this property?

We later got to know the previous owner of the bungalow. He and his wife had moved to a smaller bungalow in the village.

"Why did the new owners never move into the bungalow?" we asked.

"It was all a bit of a mystery," said Len. "A young couple viewed the bungalow. They liked what they saw and agreed to pay the asking price. The deal went through with no problems and we moved to our new bungalow. The couple never moved in. We heard they went to Spain, and it seems they never came back! We were surprised to see it put up for sale at a far higher price than we got for it!"

Before we leave the story of how we bought the bungalow ... I remember the conversation we three had after viewing it.

"The bungalow is just what we need," I had said, "but it's rather expensive."

Louie said, "We could always offer them less. We could offer £65,000."

"That would be a ridiculous offer to make," said Bill. "The owners would never drop £25,000."

Did Louie have some sort of 'hot line' to God? We called the bungalow 'Bethany' – a place where Jesus always felt at home. Later it became our retirement home. In the meantime we spent holidays there and short breaks. It was used by the family and by minister friends for holidays, and a number of couples used it for their honeymoon!

Gradually the life of the church began to settle. New people were added, but it never reached the numbers before the crisis had hit the church. It was still very vibrant, and exciting things happened, but there remained a kind of cloud over the church. Before we arrived someone in the church had a picture of a spider's web made up of separate compartments, each containing different groups of people. Another significant picture was of a sleeping beauty waiting for her prince to awaken her. Several pictures and prophecies all seemed to agree that there was a malaise.

We were due a sabbatical and it was agreed that we would have a month free of church duties and that we would spend our time exploring the problem. We examined the history of the church, talked with people who had knowledge of the church, sought help and advice from people outside the situation. We discovered that many of the previous ministers had either died during the pastorate or retired through ill health. Others had left 'under a cloud'. Throughout its life the church did have some periods of great influence, but they were short lived and never fully established. It seemed like a young child never quite reaching full growth. Consequently it lacked God's protection and was subject to the assaults of Satan. We spent some time with the previous minister who agreed with our assessment.

A Church Away Weekend was planned and we presented our findings in the form of a diagnosis of a sick person. There were five sessions: Symptoms; Case History; Diagnosis; Cure (parts 1 and 2). Part of the 'Cure' was to forgive our spiritual ancestors, loosening the church from the powers holding it back and honouring the present

faithful members who had the vision to build the present church. The folk came back referring to the church as "the New Church of the Redeemer". The whole spirit in the church improved from that time on.

The demands of the church began to take their toll. We felt drained. We had absorbed a lot of the hurts that people had shared with us and we were beginning to feel the strain. We felt we had done what God had called us to do. The powers of darkness had been met head-on and the church reclaimed for Christ. There was a greater sense of unity in the church and a happier spirit. The way was open now for someone else to build up the church free from the hindrances of the past. We shared how we felt with the Area Superintendent and he agreed with us that it would be right for us to move to another pastorate where we could have a reasonable length of ministry before retiring. He put our names forward at the Superintendents Meeting indicating that we were seeking another pastorate. The Area Superintendent from Yorkshire, who knew us from our time there, immediately said, "I want them for Clayton."

We had been in Birmingham for four difficult years. We had learned a great deal. We had wonderful support from the charismatic Baptist Ministers in the area who met regularly in our house. Many in the church supported us and regularly met with us to pray for us. We made many lovely friends who continued to visit us when we eventually retired. We were sad in many ways to leave Birmingham, but we were looking forward to the new challenge. Many ministers getting near to retirement have difficulty in finding a pastorate, but the Lord was gracious to us in leading the Church at Clayton to call us. We looked forward to being back in West Yorkshire where we had spent so many happy years before and after marriage.

14

"Those who survive the wind live a long life"

We visited the church at Clayton in the January. Before going to meet the Deacons and to "preach with a view" we spent a couple of days near Leyburn in North Yorkshire. We wanted to take some time praying that we would recognise the Lord's will regarding this church. Clayton was not unknown to us. In our time in Huddersfield I had shared the leadership of the very successful Annual Youth Week organised by the Yorkshire Baptist Association (the YBA) with David Richardson, the Minister at Clayton. This had entailed coming to Clayton for planning meetings. Bill had preached at Clayton on a couple of occasions.

Like Longley, Clayton was a hilly situation. It was on the edge of Bradford but was in fact much older and had only become officially part of the city in the 1930s. The Brontë Way footpath passed through the village leading to Haworth just a few miles away. The Brontë children had been born in the village of Thornton, a mile or two from Clayton.

The Area Superintendent had told us that the church had gone through a difficult time in the last few years. After a period of growth under the ministry of David Richardson, which included building a new church to replace the old large chapel, problems arose. David had moved on and a new minister had come, and some felt dissatisfied with his leadership. A group broke away

from the church and set up in the Village Hall as the "true church". The minister, after only a short time, was asked to leave. The Area Superintendent had taken the church under his wing, but with little success. The Association Missioner and then the Association Secretary also tried to bring healing. These godly and gifted men were too busy to give the time the situation needed. Joe Wieland, a wise and gifted retired minister, gave part-time leadership that settled the depleted congregation and prepared them for full-time ministry. The Area Superintendent felt that our experience of dealing with the wounded church in Birmingham and also our understanding of the Yorkshire temperament would fit us for this difficult task.

As we travelled to Clayton snow fell and travel conditions became very difficult. At one point on a country road our car skidded, but we managed to keep it under control. We were glad to reach Clayton and were warmly received by the deacons. There were now only three deacons, all strong in the faith and having true 'Yorkshire grit'. They welcomed us warmly and we spent a good session with them. With complete honesty they related the story of the church. We were instantly drawn to these men. The Area Superintendent had told them of our experience in Birmingham and also that we were due to retire in four years or so.

We had a good day with the church on the Sunday. As well as taking the services we met the people in a more informal way. We had a tour round the village seeing the old houses, some back-to-back houses from the days when the woollen mill functioned. The old mill was now the head office of the Wool Marketing Board. Many footpaths criss-crossed the village and we could see how pastoral visiting benefited from knowing the various ways through the labyrinth. There was a large council estate and a park and also a lot of new housing. There were shops in the centre and the Village Hall. We saw the two other churches in the village, Anglican and Methodist. It was a popular place to live, being on the edge of the country yet only three miles from the heart of Bradford. We also

spent some time with Joe and Mary Wieland whom we knew from when we were in Yorkshire. Everything was very positive.

The church meeting later in the week discussed and prayed about our visit, and as a result they invited us to be joint Ministers of the Church. One of the things they stated was that they would put a stair lift in the Manse for Aunt Louie should we choose to accept the call. We prayed this through and felt the Lord saying that we should accept the invitation.

Interestingly, Bill remembered something that had happened some years before when he preached at Clayton. It was at the time when we were seeking the Lord's guidance about moving from Longley. The church at Clayton had not yet appointed a successor to David Richardson. As Bill was leading the service he heard an inner voice say, "I want you to minister in this church". He was concentrating on leading the service, so he pushed the thought aside. The Church Secretary made an announcement to the church during the service to say that their invitation to a minister had been accepted. Bill's reaction was, "Bill, you've got your wires crossed. This is not where the Lord is guiding you." This experience was only recalled by Bill after we had felt the Lord calling us to accept the invitation from Clayton. It served as further evidence that the Lord was indeed calling us to Clayton.

The people were mainly solid West Yorkshire stock – reliable, faithful and 'calling a spade a spade'. We quickly grew to love them. Historically, the people of Clayton were known for their longevity and there were many people in their eighties living very active lives. It was considered that the secret lay in the hilly situation and the constant wind. "The wind always blows here. Those who survive the wind live a long life."

We arrived in early May. A few weeks later it was Pentecost Sunday and I made an appeal at the end of the service for people to come forward to be filled with the Holy Spirit. Seven came forward, amongst them an elderly lady. I had the joy of baptising her some weeks later.

Not long after we settled in Clayton the Annual Meeting of the Yorkshire Baptist Association took place. As was the custom there was a point when new Ministers in the area were formally welcomed. Because of our years in Huddersfield we were well known to many. What was a particular joy to us was that also being welcomed was our daughter Liz. She had been accepted for Ministerial Training at the Northern Baptist College and part of her training involved the student pastorate at the West Vale Baptist Church near Halifax. Comments were made about "the family business"!

From the start we sought to encourage love in the Fellowship and a spirit of forgiveness towards those who had split away from the church. The group no longer met in the village hall and they seemed to be wandering around looking for places where they felt at home; but they found none. Gradually they came back into the life of the church. All but one young couple who had left the village eventually returned. It was good to see how those who had stayed accepted them back without any reference to the split. They were welcomed as brothers and sisters in Christ. One became the Church Secretary. The leader of the group was the last to come back. Bill had the joy of baptising him shortly before we retired.

There was a lot of musical ability in the church and we formed a very able music group to lead the worship. There was a growing junior church and family services were very exciting. House Groups met in a number of homes. Soon we were able to appoint more deacons, and various people took on all sorts of responsibilities.

A short while before we left Longley I had been sent by the church to Ilkley to train to run a 'Masterlife' Course. This was a very good system for developing disciples. I had never been able to use it in Birmingham, but we saw it was ideal for the people at Clayton. I was able to take quite a number through the year-long course. It was good to see how they became very strong in the Lord. One of those who was particularly helped by the course was an elderly lady called Vera. She received a new zest for life and became 'on fire' for the Lord. She became a great friend of Aunt Louie, sharing a like zeal for

the Lord.

There were a number of very interesting characters in the church. George had been a painter and decorator for many years. He and his wife had been stalwarts in the church for many years. He told of how some years ago he was painting inside the old church. He had placed the ladder against the gallery and proceeded to paint some kind of ornamented decoration.

"When I finished painting one of the fancy bits," he said, "I wanted to study the quality of my work, so I stepped back off the ladder to look! The amazing thing is that I didn't fall! I swear that God held me up!"

I'm sure that God did so. George was not given to telling fancy tales. He had experienced a wonderful intervention by God. He lived well into his nineties and was greatly loved.

Albert was another true Yorkshire man – frank yet gentle. He had been a fine athlete in his youth as a middle distance runner. The war came and he was called up. He was rescued at Dunkirk and then sent to Singapore. The day after he arrived there the Japanese captured Singapore and Albert was sent with others to a notorious camp. His basic fitness helped him to endure the horrible treatment he received. He survived his four close friends who, one by one, died in dreadful circumstances. He buried each of them. He was forced to race against some of his captors despite his poor physical condition. He was disembowelled and suffered from severe malnutrition. He survived the war but was in very poor health. For the rest of his life he had to have special care.

The wonderful thing about Albert was that he bore no malice towards his captors. "It was my faith that kept me going," he said. "The Japanese lads were themselves brutalised by their officers. I was sorry for them. They didn't know the love of a wife as I did. They didn't know Jesus." Albert didn't talk much about his experience in the war and we felt very privileged that he shared this with us.

I started a banner group and our first banner was "He has made

me glad!" It became a favourite for quite a number. In time we had so many banners that they were changed Sunday by Sunday to suit the theme of the day. We made a special banner for a Yorkshire Baptist Association Rally in York Minster. It declared, "Go into all the world". Many of the banners were very ambitious. We had a group of banners suspended from the ceiling depicting the Fruit of the Spirit.

On one Church Away Day we looked at the findings of a survey of 500 people who had been asked how they became Christians. It was discovered that while there were many factors in bringing people to Christ, the one that stood out most was the effectiveness of 'friendship evangelism'. People turn to Christ through seeing Him and His love in their friends. We developed this in our House Groups and it became a fundamental aspect of the church life. One of the ways this friendship evangelism was developed was on Bonfire Night. The church had a lot of ground and there was an ideal site for holding a bonfire. The village was invited to share in the fun. Fireworks were carefully controlled with only selected people setting them off at a roped-off area. It became the central bonfire celebration for the village with about 200 people enjoying the family fun and the fireworks. A good supper was enjoyed by those who came.

Bill and I were regularly asked to take assemblies in the First School. This was always a very enjoyable occasion and we loved being able to meet with the children. On one occasion when Bill was visiting the school he saw two children who were obviously working through a computer programme about Vikings. Bill chatted with them and told them that he was descended from the Vikings. As he left them he heard one say to the other, "He's a REAL Viking!"

Every year the Middle School asked if they could bring the top classes to visit the church building and learn about the history and beliefs of the Baptists. I was glad to have this time with the children. First I talked to them about the history of the church and the basic beliefs of Baptists. In groups I demonstrated in the open dry

baptistry how and why we baptised believers. This always fascinated the children because it was so different from the infant baptism most of them knew about. While I spoke about baptism the others roamed around the building answering some set questions and making various notes and drawings. The children also visited the Methodist and Anglican churches in the village.

We had very good relationships with the Anglican and Methodist Churches. We met regularly with the Ministers. One outcome of our meetings was to feel led to have a united mission to the village. The three churches agreed to do this and invited Robin Gamble, the Missioner for the Bradford Anglican Diocese, to lead it. He brought two other clergy to share in the leadership. It was a very fruitful week. One successful event was the Pub Quiz made up of half Christians and half non-Christians. After the fun of the quiz Robin said, "I have two questions to ask each of you. 'Why are you here?' and 'Where are you going?'." The challenge was clear and powerful.

Another interesting event during that week that attracted many people was the evening entitled, "The Gospel According to the Beatles." It was a multi-media presentation using music from the Beatles. The first part was fairly light hearted with a quiz, and then after some supper the presentation became more serious. Particularly powerful was the use of mime artistes who used 'The Fool on the Hill' to bring home the message of the Cross and a slide presentation to link 'The Long and Winding Road' with the challenge of where our lives were leading. It was a moving experience and spoke powerfully to the unchurched people especially.

Louie's general health deteriorated. She had a number of spells in hospital and during one such time the doctor said she needed 24-hour care and advised that she should go into a nursing home. We talked it over with Louie and she saw the wisdom of this. We were able to get her into an excellent nursing home in Clayton. She settled in very well and found real friends there. They gathered daily in the conservatory where Louie could enjoy the sunshine. There was intelligent conversation, real friendship, time for talking and time for reading. I visited her every second day and Bill also frequently visited her. From time to time we took her out for special occasions. Many of the church people visited her and Vera was especially regular. She and Louie enjoyed rich fellowship and friendship.

Gradually the Fellowship grew. More adults, young couples and children came and a wonderful family sense grew within the fellowship that drew others to attend church. I think particularly of a recently-married young couple who moved into the village and rented a house. They had just started new jobs in the area and wanted to settle where there was a good church. They started in Clayton and tried the Baptist Church first. They felt 'at home' right from the start and looked no further! They bought a house and became valued members, particularly working amongst the young people. They were to experience great support from the fellowship when their first child was born with a serious condition that required many visits to St James' Hospital in Leeds. He survived the first difficult years and was wonderfully able, through medical care and prayer, to grow up to live a happy and healthy life.

The church attendance grew so that we began to think in terms of somehow extending the building. We reorganised the seating to accommodate as many as possible. Because we were nearing retirement it was clear that this would be something for a future minister to deal with. We were glad that the church had found healing and was growing. We gave the church nine months' notice of our retirement. We encouraged them to seek a future minister while we were still with them. It was important that there should be as little gap as possible between our leaving and a successor starting.

I discussed the matter of our retirement with Louie. "When Bill and I retire and go to Highley, will you come with us? You know there's a lovely nursing home near our bungalow and we will be able to visit you as we do here."

"I don't know what to do. I'm so happy here. I've lovely friends in the home. Dear friends like Vera visit me regularly. It would be such an upheaval to move; and yet I love Highley and I love being with my

151

dear ones. I would miss sitting by the lovely pampas grass, listening to the birds and enjoying the sun. I just don't know what to decide."

"Louie, we want the best for you and Bill and I will fit in with your wishes," I said. "If you choose to stay in Clayton, we will visit you regularly and we know the church family here will do so as well. Should you choose to come to Highley that will suit us too."

When I visited Louie just shortly before we left Clayton she said she was not feeling too well. When she felt well she would sometimes rather whimsically ask, "Do you think I'll get my telegram from the Queen?" When she didn't feel on top she would ask, not in a morbid way, "Do you think I'm dying?" On this occasion the question was asked, "Do you think I'm dying?"

To jolly her up I said, "You can't die yet. You know Bill and I are going to Canada for a special holiday. We want to be able to tell you all about our visit. If you take ill while we're away we'll come back at once."

"I wouldn't want to spoil your holiday," she answered. "I'm sure the Lord will organise things for me. I'll either die before you go or after you come back."

The Saturday before our last weekend we invited people to come to our house for tea and refreshments. We had always encouraged folk to come to the Manse, and this was a last opportunity to share hospitality. Since our bungalow in Highley was furnished we had a lot of furniture and other household things for which we had no further use. All manner of things were marked for sale. The money raised we gave to the church to buy more chairs for the growing congregation. A very sizeable amount was raised.

As the time of our last Sunday drew near, Jo, the Church Secretary, told us to keep the last Saturday free, but gave no details. We expected some kind of farewell, but had no idea what form it would take. When the day arrived Jo rang us and said, "Don't come to the church until your escort arrives for you." "Escort"? We only lived 100 yards from the church!

Our escort came and we walked to the church wondering just

what lay in store. We didn't want any fuss, but we did want to enjoy being with our church family at this important time in our lives. We arrived to find the church filled to its absolute capacity. All our five children were there and their families. We saw my brother Dave and his wife Meg. There were friends from the churches where we had ministered in over 38 years.

We were ushered up to the platform. We looked around and saw representatives from local churches, the Bradford District of Baptist Churches and the YBA. It so happened that earlier in the week we had attended a Bradford District Meeting and had said our farewells to them. We had been surprised at the rather half-hearted comments at that time. Now we knew why! Jo had instructed all the invited people, including our family, that there was to be absolute secrecy about the nature of this Saturday evening event. No one had dropped the slightest hint! To keep maximum secrecy Jo and his wife Caroline were the only ones who knew the whole programme and in this way maintained a high level of secrecy. Our children had hidden their cars in case we recognised them on the way to the church and they had made their own arrangements for accommodation.

The whole event was led superbly by Jo, who kept it from degenerating into a 'back-slapping' event, which is something we did not want. It was an evening of fun and love. The music group sang a song based on the Beatles' 'When I'm 64'. The favourite church banner, "He has made me glad" was brought in and the song of this text was sung. Another was brought in, "He has made me Bill"! Various greetings were given by people from the churches we had pastored, the YBA, the Bradford Baptist Churches, the Clayton churches. There were letters and videos from those unable to come. The Clayton members were very generous in giving us gifts. The evening was rounded off by everyone making their way to the school hall next door to the church where outside caterers organised a wonderful meal for all the church and visitors to enjoy. The whole event was one of the happiest days of our lives and we praise God for

153

the way the whole affair was handled by Jo and Caroline.

The last Sunday was a good day of worship. The Presence of the Lord was very real and the love of the people overwhelming. The next day we made our way to Highley. To celebrate our retirement we planned to go to Canada for three weeks and visit Bill's sister Dorothy who lived in the Rockies in the south of British Columbia. Our plan was to come back to Clayton the next weekend to visit Louie in the nursing home and then fly to Canada the following Thursday.

I received a phone call from the manager of the nursing home on the Friday. "I'm very sorry to have to tell you that your Aunt Louie died just after nine o'clock this morning."

"What happened? I saw her just a few days ago and she seemed her usual self. My husband and I were planning to come and see her tomorrow."

"It was totally unexpected. She had had a good night's sleep. Two nursing assistants gave her a bath prior to dressing her. She enjoyed her bath and was joking with the nurses as they dried her when she just closed her eyes and died! The nurses did what they could but to no avail. I am so sorry. She was a lovely lady."

"Thank you for calling me. I appreciate all that you have done for Louie. My husband and I will drive up straight away." We rushed to Clayton.

The suddenness of Louie's death put aside our anticipation of going to Canada. We were able to make the arrangements for her funeral. I remembered Louie's words as we talked about whether she would stay in Clayton or come down to Highley. "I'm sure the Lord will organise it for me. I'll either die before you go or after you come back." With gentleness the Lord called her home. The funeral took place the day before we flew to Canada. Louie was 98. How privileged I was to have known her. She taught me about serving the Lord, especially in my younger days. Ruth and her children William and Eleanor represented the family. Dave and Meg were there. Cousin Charlie came down from the Highlands. Two very significant chapters of my life ended at the same time – the influence of my aunt and our working days in the full-time ministry.

Conclusion

"**S**aved for a purpose"? As a child I had wondered what that meant. Now I knew. Saved to be Bill's wife. I had been sure of that from the moment God said, "Marry Bill." Saved to be the mother of our five children – what a privilege, what a responsibility, but of that too I was sure. But saved, also, to be a minister serving God in the local community, preaching, pastoring and reaching out to others with the love of God.

Who is worthy of such a calling? No one is, but He has promised to give all the grace that such a calling requires. As a teenager, shy and even afraid to speak to people I recognised in the street, I resolved that if God would show me His plans, that was all I needed. I didn't need to know if I would fulfil them. If God called, He would equip. I have found it to be so and it has become a life principle for me.

Bill and I are retired. The Lord continues to open up new avenues of service. "Oh God, if there is a God, show Yourself to me" had been the prayer uttered many times beside baby Harry's grave. God did show Himself to me and has continued to show Himself to me in so many different ways. One day I shall see Him face to face. What a joy that will be to enter into the fullness of God's purpose for my life.